austerlitz 1805

the fate of empires

Library of Congress Cataloging-in-Publication Data

Castle, Ian.
   Austerlitz 1805 : the fate of empires / Ian Castle.
      p. cm. – (Praeger illustrated military history, ISSN 1547-206X)
   Originally published: London: Osprey, 2002.
   Includes bibliographical references and index.
   ISBN 0-275-98619-5 (alk. paper)
   1. Austerlitz, Battle of, Czech Republic, 1805.2. Napoleonic Wars, 1800-1815 –
Campaigns – Czech Republic. I. Title. II. Series
   DC227.5.A8C37   2005
   940.2'742'043724 – dc22   2004061727

British Library Cataloguing in Publication Data is available.

First published in paperback in 2002 by Osprey Publishing Limited,
Midland House, West Way, Botley, Oxford OX2 0PH, UK
443 Park Avenue South, New York, NY 10016, USA
All rights reserved.

Copyright © 2005 by Osprey Publishing Limited

Library of Congress Catalog Card Number: 2004061727
ISBN: 0-275-98619-5
ISSN: 1547-206X

Praeger Publishers, 88 Post Road West, Westport, CT 06881
An imprint of Greenwood Publishing Group, Inc.
www.praeger.com

Printed in China through World Print Ltd.

The paper used in this book complies with the Permanent Paper Standard issued
by the National Information Standards Organization (Z39.48-1984).

10 9 8 7 6 5 4 3 2 1

IAN CASTLE

austerlitz 1805

the fate of empires

Praeger Illustrated Military History Series

PRAEGER

Westport, Connecticut
London

CONTENTS

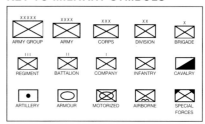

KEY TO MILITARY SYMBOLS

XXXXX ARMY GROUP	XXXX ARMY	XXX CORPS	XX DIVISION	X BRIGADE
III REGIMENT	II BATTALION	I COMPANY	INFANTRY	CAVALRY
ARTILLERY	ARMOUR	MOTORIZED	AIRBORNE	SPECIAL FORCES

FOREWORD

I wrote *Austerlitz 1805 – Battle of the Three Emperors* eleven years ago; one of the first pair of titles published in the new Osprey Campaign series. As Hon. Consultant Editor I was pleased by the popularity of the series. Since 1990 Osprey's Campaign books have continued from strength to strength, and now include over 100 titles by numerous military historians on a range of battles. Over the intervening years there has been the opportunity for more research and a number of new writers have emerged. By looking again at classic military engagements from fresh angles they are adding to our previous understanding of these great battles. Ian Castle is one of these writers. By chance I shared with him a visit to Vienna and Czechoslovakia in August 1989 with members of the Napoleonic Association, a visit that included trips to the battlefields of Aspern-Essling and Austerlitz. It was this that inspired him to begin his research. Since then Ian has contributed two very useful volumes to the Campaign series on the battles of Aspern-Essling and Eggmuhl. These have added to our greater understanding of the Austrian involvement in these campaigns, an area that had previously been under explored in the English language. Now I am sure our readers will enjoy his new *Austerlitz 1805 – The Fate of Empires*. After all, as Professor Pieter Geyl of Holland once said: 'History is indeed an argument without end'.

David G. Chandler.

Dr. David G. Chandler, September 2001

THE ROAD TO WAR

O n 9 November 1805 the Lord Mayor of London acclaimed William Pitt, British Prime Minister and sworn enemy of Napoleonic France, as the 'the saviour of Europe'. The recent news of Nelson's destruction of the Franco-Spanish fleet at Trafalgar had been the cause of great rejoicing. In response, Pitt realistically declared 'Europe is not to be saved by any single man. England has saved herself by her exertions, and will, as I trust, save Europe by her example.' Twelve weeks later Pitt was dead and the armies of Austria and Russia, two of Europe's great powers, lay defeated. One man stood pre-eminent across the continent – Napoleon Bonaparte, Emperor of the French and King of Italy.

The path to war that led to the frosty Moravian countryside on 2 December 1805 began with the death of the Second Coalition. This wide-ranging alliance between Britain, Austria, Russia, Naples and Turkey was finally laid to rest at Amiens in 1802, although if anyone expected a protracted period of peace to follow they were to be disappointed.

Following the coup of 1799 Bonaparte became First Consul, a title confirmed for life in 1802. The monarchs of the old European order looked on suspiciously as this soldier-statesman began work to bring stability back to France.

Inevitably, the peace was short-lived. Fourteen months after Britain and France signed the Peace of Amiens, with relations between the two

The Peace of Amiens, signed on 25 March 1802, was initially greeted with great joy in Paris and London. Yet the respite was brief and just over a year later the two countries were at war once again. (Musée Frédéric Masson – Sammlung Alfred und Roland Umhey)

countries rapidly deteriorating, France placed an embargo on British shipping in French ports, to which Britain responded by declaring war. Manipulating evidence of Bonaparte's territorial ambitions – as demonstrated by his annexation of Piedmont and the French presence in Hanover, Holland and Switzerland – Britain agitated in Europe against France. Meanwhile, Bonaparte ordered a vast concentration of the army along the English Channel coastline as he planned to rid himself of what he saw as the constant treachery of Britain. In response Britain called out the Militia and strengthened her Navy.

However, one final spark was required to re-ignite the flames of a European war. Many Royalist opponents to Bonaparte's regime were conspiring, supported by British money, to secure the restoration of the Bourbon royal family. Reports of the activities of one of these Royalists, the Duke of Enghien, had reached the ear of Bonaparte, and determined to put an end to plots against himself and his family he ordered the arrest of the Duke. The little matter that he resided in the neutral territory of Baden seemed to be of no consequence. Kidnapped and taken to the Château de Vincennes, he was charged with treason, summarily tried, found guilty and executed. The great ruling dynasties of Europe were outraged.

As the situation in Europe undeniably took a turn for the worse there was great public clamour in Britain for the return of William Pitt as Prime Minister. Pitt, a great opponent of French expansion, had resigned in 1801. His policies had attacked France's trade and her colonies while financing her opponents in Europe. Now with war apparently inevitable, Pitt returned to office in May 1804, a few weeks after the Enghien affair. The man that had done much to construct the First and Second Coalitions against France set to with a will to create a third. In November 1804, Russia and Austria agreed a preliminary treaty indicating their determination to work together and pursue joint war plans. The proclamation earlier, in May 1804, declaring Bonaparte as Emperor of the French added to the urgency of their endeavours to seek a satisfactory alliance. At his coronation on 2 December 1804, Emperor Napoleon, as Bonaparte had now become, symbolically placed the crown upon his own head amidst great pomp and ceremony. Five months later he added King of Italy to his titles – a move guaranteed to alienate Austria even further.

OPPOSING PLANS

While the senior military officers of Austria and Russia discussed plans of war, the Russian Tsar, Alexander, opened discussions with Britain. In April 1805 the two governments reached agreement and signed an alliance. British financial subsidies to both Russia and Austria agreed during these discussions were finalised without any representatives of the Austrian government being present. This added fuel to the protests of those, led by the War Minister Archduke Charles, who doubted the reliability of Russian promises and felt that the army was as yet unprepared for another war. Austria prevaricated and it was not until August 1805 that the Third Coalition was formalised, with Britain, Russia, Austria as well as Sweden and Naples united against France. Allied efforts to bring Prussia into the coalition stalled as France attempted to win Prussian support too. Initially King Frederick William III advocated a policy of neutrality – when he did finally decide to side with the Allies it was too late.

Work began immediately to agree the grand strategy of the campaign. Driven on by Russia the plan called for an unprecedented Europe-wide advance against France and her recent territorial acquisitions. From the shores of the Baltic in the north to the heel of Italy in the south, numerous multinational armies, numbering half a million men, would advance and sweep the French away. A joint force of Russians and Swedes with British support would occupy Hanover and be in a position to threaten Holland. Three Russian armies were to operate in central Europe. The most northerly of these, commanded by Bennigsen, was to advance from Russia through Bohemia with orders to keep an eye on the Prussians while protecting the right flank of the main Russian army led by Kutuzov. His force was to march through Austria to Bavaria where it would link up with the Austrian army nominally commanded by Archduke Ferdinand, although FML Mack actually exercised command. Behind Kutuzov came a third Russian army, led by Buxhöwden, which would be able to support either Kutuzov or Bennigsen as required. To the south of this great concentration in Bavaria an Austrian force commanded by Archduke John would hold the Tyrol, enabling communications to be maintained with northern Italy. It was here that the main Austrian force would assemble, under the command of Archduke Charles, with orders to march westwards and sweep the French from Lombardy. Then, co-operating with the Austro-Russian forces in Bavaria, he would join the push towards France. On the southernmost flank of the offensive an unlikely mixed force of Russians, British and Neapolitans was to combine and advance up the spine of Italy. It was hoped that as the grand strategy gained momentum additional troops would become available as Bavaria and other German states recognised the wind of change, and threw in their lot with the Allies. On paper the

THE STRATEGIC PLANS OF THE THIRD COALITION

plans looked impressive. However, the co-ordination of such a massive enterprise was beyond the capabilities of the Allies. The eventual declaration of neutrality by Prussia and Bavaria's secret alliance with France were to deny the Allies many of the troops they had hoped for. In addition, disputes within the Austrian military hierarchy about the army's readiness for war and the strategy to be employed, coupled with last minute army reforms, did not auger well for a successful conclusion of the campaign.

Inevitably, a scheme of this size could not hope to evade discovery by Napoleon's network of spies. The main strength of the French army was encamped along the Channel coast preparing for an invasion of England. This enterprise had been endlessly delayed by the inability of the French navy to gain mastery of the Channel long enough to enable Napoleon to transport his army across the thin strip of water. Now a great threat had manifested itself to the east. On the same day that Kutuzov commenced his march westwards from the Russian-Galician border, Napoleon ordered the first of his formations to depart from their coastal encampments and march eastwards for the Rhine. Far ahead of Kutuzov, the unsupported Austrian army led by Ferdinand and Mack had crossed the Inn River into Bavaria on 8 September and pushed on towards Ulm. The Austrians had anticipated that the Bavarian army would join forces with them and so were somewhat dismayed when the Bavarians withdrew having already concluded an alliance with Napoleon. The scene was now set for one of the great manoeuvres of the Napoleonic era – the encirclement of Ulm. At one stroke the plans of the Third Coalition were to be destroyed and its armies thrown into retreat.

CHRONOLOGY

1802

25 March 1802 Peace of Amiens

1 August 1802 Napoleon proclaimed First Consul for life

2 August 1802 France annexes Elba

2 September 1802 France annexes Piedmont

15 October 1802 France invades Switzerland

1803

5 May 1803 France places an embargo on British ships using French ports

18 May 1803 Britain declares war on France

1 June 1803 France occupies Hanover

15 June 1803 French army moves into camps along the Channel coast

1804

14 March 1804 Kidnapping of the Duke of Enghien

21 March 1804 Execution of the Duke of Enghien

18 May 1804 Napoleon proclaimed Emperor

6 November 1804 Austria and Russia sign a preliminary treaty

2 December 1804 Coronation of Napoleon in Paris

1805

11 April 1805 Alliance signed between Britain and Russia

26 May 1805 Napoleon crowns himself King of Italy

4 June 1805 France annexes Genoa

9 August 1805 Austria joins Britain and Russia in Third Coalition

25 August 1805 Napoleon orders army from coastal camps to the Rhine

25 August 1805 Kutuzov's Russian army commences march to join Austrians

5 September 1805 Austrian army advances from Wels

8 September 1805 Austrians enter Bavaria

25 September 1805 French army cross the Rhine

7 October 1805 First French units reach the Danube at Donauwörth

8 October 1805 Battle of Wertingen

11 October 1805 Battle of Haslach

14 October 1805 Battle of Elchingen

20 October 1805 Mack surrenders Austrian army at Ulm

21 October 1805 Combined fleets of France and Spain defeated at Battle of Trafalgar by British fleet under Lord Nelson

26 October 1805 French army begins pursuit of Kutuzov

28–31 October 1805 Battle of Caldiero in northern Italy

30 October 1805 Allied rearguard action at Ried

31 October 1805 Allied rearguard action at Lambach

4 November 1805 Austrian rearguard action at Steyr

5 November 1805 Allied rearguard action at Amstetten

8 November 1805 Austrians defeated at Mariazell

9 November 1805 Kutuzov crosses to the north bank of the Danube

11 November 1805 Battle of Dürnstein

12 November 1805 French troops enter Vienna

13 November 1805 French capture bridges across the Danube

16 November 1805 Battle of Hollabrünn/Schöngrabern

18–22 November 1805 Allies regroup and retreat to Olmütz

20 November 1805 Napoleon halts the French pursuit at Brünn

20 November 1805 Cavalry clash at Raussnitz

24 November 1805 Allies decide to fight

25 November 1805 Russian Imperial Guard joins army at Olmütz

27 November 1805 Allies commence advance

28 November 1805 Allies take Wischau and advance to Raussnitz

28 November 1805 Napoleon orders French army to concentrate east of Brünn

30 November–1 Dec Allies occupy Pratzen heights

2 December 1805 Battle of Austerlitz

OPPOSING COMMANDERS

Emperor Napoleon

It was in 1796 that Europe first became familiar with the name of General Bonaparte. It was then that he took command of the unpaid, ill-supplied and demoralised Army of Italy. Bonaparte arrived like a whirlwind, reorganised the army with the help of his chief of staff, Louis Berthier, inspired his men and led them against the Piedmontese and Austrians. Brushing aside the Piedmontese he drove the Austrians back on Mantua. Having thwarted attempts to relieve the city, the Austrian army retreated after the Battle of Rivoli. Bonaparte pursued, and, without waiting for the authority of the Directory, forced them to accept his terms for peace in April 1797. The subsequent Treaty of Campo Formio established the Cisalpine Republic from lands Bonaparte had captured in Lombardy. Before he was finished, he had organised its government and proclaimed a constitution, an extraordinary achievement for an officer of the army.

Bonaparte was welcomed back in Paris as a national hero. Those men who had fought for him had learnt to admire him as a great leader and, perhaps more importantly, as one who managed to pay them and bring them victory in battle. Bonaparte learnt the great political value of military glory and had the opportunity to develop his ideas of warfare in the field. Meanwhile the Directory learnt that here was a man who had the support of the people and who could be a potential danger in the future.

Rewarded for this success with the command of the Army of England, Bonaparte soon realised that the planned conquest of England was impractical while the Royal Navy dominated the Channel. Instead, he advocated an attack on Egypt that would damage Britain's trade with India and the Middle East, leading to the advent of a new French empire of the east. The Directory was enthusiastic about the plan, if nothing else it would take Bonaparte away from Paris. The Egyptian campaign got under way in May 1798, but the French army suffered mixed fortunes. News reached Bonaparte in Egypt of the defeats inflicted on France by the Second Coalition and of the weakness of the Directory. Bonaparte determined to leave his army in Egypt and return to France. Back in Paris in October 1799, it was clear he had lost none of his popularity. In November a coup d'état established Bonaparte as

In December 1804 First Consul Bonaparte became Napoleon, Emperor of the French. Five months later, much to the consternation of Europe's ruling dynasties, he added the crown of Italy.

one of three consuls who would govern France, though he eventually emerged as First Consul, the de facto ruler of France. From this position of power Bonaparte led the army against the Austrians once more and defeated them in a very close-run battle at Marengo in May 1800. A further French victory at Hohenlinden eventually led to the Treaty of Amiens in 1802.

Bonaparte hoped for a period of peace following Amiens during which he could stabilise France. He set about introducing a vast programme of cultural, social, civil and religious reforms, but all the time his hatred of Britain remained undiminished. With relations between the two countries teetering on the edge, Bonaparte created a new army, *La Grande Armée*, which he stationed along the Channel coast and prepared for an invasion of England. However, this highly trained and motivated army was never to cross the Channel and march on London, instead it was destined to sweep across Europe to do battle with the armies of Austria and Russia. This time they would not be led into battle by First Consul Bonaparte; this time the man who was to inspire them was Napoleon, Emperor of the French.

Emperor (Tsar) Alexander I

Alexander was born in 1777, son of the obsessive and fanatical future Tsar, Paul I, and grandson of Catherine the Great. Catherine, placing little trust in her son Paul, exerted great influence on Alexander's upbringing, hoping he would succeed her. However, following Catherine's death in 1796, Paul became Tsar although there were many at the Russian Court who opposed his reign. Five years later, in 1801, Paul's assassination following a palace coup saw Alexander installed as Tsar in his place. The new Tsar, head of the House of Romanov, was 23 years of age.

As a ruler Alexander showed many positive qualities and embarked on a series of reforms that saw the creation of eight new ministries, bringing a more orderly administration to government. He promoted education and also went some way to improving the condition of the Russian serfs but could not abolish the institution. Alexander had grace, charm and spoke French well. Even Napoleon took to him. He once described Alexander as, 'young, friendly, and very good looking; and he has more intelligence than is commonly supposed.' Others, however, considered Alexander unstable.

Initially Alexander observed Bonaparte's progress with interest and believed his success could bring stability to a France thrown into turmoil by revolution, but he quickly changed his views. Having grown up under the influence of Catherine his determination to establish Russia as the grand arbiter of Europe grew, until he saw himself as the one man who could restore peace.

Alexander was vain and impressionable and at court he surrounded himself with a circle of young, confident, aggressive and arrogant aides-de-camp, to the exclusion of more mature, experienced and cautious officers. These men appealed to his vanity and encouraged him to over-confidence. In military matters he was naïve and inexperienced, but under the influence of these flatterers he saw it as his duty to lead his army in the defence of Europe from French aggression.

As First Consul, Bonaparte made a number of overtures to Alexander to secure Russian support against Britain but failed each time.

Tsar Alexander I came to the throne in 1801 and determined to establish Russia as the great arbiter of Europe. To oppose French expansion Russia joined with Austria and Britain and worked aggressively towards the formation of a Third Coalition.

Continuing French activity in Germany, Italy and the Mediterranean appeared designed to provoke the anger of both Russia and Austria. With the Enghien affair, Alexander felt Napoleon had gone too far. Now was the time to destroy Napoleon and return the Bourbons to their throne. Bringing Britain and Austria together with Russia, Alexander sowed the seeds of the Third Coalition and dreamt of fulfilling his destiny, bringing peace to war-ravaged Europe. Although he lacked any experience of battle, Alexander was to assume supreme command of the Allied forces at the climactic confrontation at Austerlitz.

Emperor Francis I (Kaiser Franz I)

Francis was born in 1768, the same year as Napoleon Bonaparte, in Florence. His father was the future Emperor Leopold II. Francis received some military training, then in 1786, his uncle, Emperor Joseph II, sent him on a military tour of the Habsburg kingdoms of Bohemia and Hungary. Two years later he visited the Turkish front and in 1789 was present at the capture of Belgrade. Joseph died in 1790, leaving the throne to Francis's father, Leopold II. However, Leopold's reign was brief and in 1792 Francis became head of the House of Habsburg as Francis II, Holy Roman Emperor and King of Bohemia and Hungary. Almost immediately Francis found Austria at war with revolutionary France, it would be 23 years before peace fully returned to his empire.

Francis was an absolutist and firmly believed in his duty to maintain the Habsburg dynasty as a major power in Europe. He was not a great leader but he was popular with his people. His application and sense of duty and justice had earned him praise from Joseph II, but he was also criticised for being stubborn and lacking imagination.

Emperor Francis I succeeded his father to the Habsburg throne in 1792 and almost immediately became embroiled in the Revolutionary Wars against France. Francis was no military leader but the terms of the alliance with Russia required him to take the field in 1805.

The subsequent wars against the French were disastrous for Austria. Forced to accept harsh peace terms in 1797 and again in 1801, Austria lost vast tracts of territory but developed a burning desire for revenge – the only question was when. In the meantime, Francis took advantage of Napoleon's decision to crown himself Emperor to attempt to strengthen his own position. The power and glories of the Holy Roman Empire, long since undermined, diminished further as Napoleon's incursions and involvement along the Rhine increased. Francis took the opportunity to consolidate his power in Austria, Bohemia, Hungary and northern Italy, renouncing the title Francis II of the Holy Roman Empire in August 1804 and proclaiming himself Francis I Emperor of Austria.

The approaching war of the Third Coalition put Francis in a peculiar situation. At a meeting of the Russian and Austrian staff, the Russians had stipulated that their main army, commanded by Kutuzov, was to be subordinate only to Emperor Francis and Archduke Charles, Austria's nominal War Minister. Kutuzov would not accept orders from any other Austrian general. With Charles commanding in northern Italy, Francis of necessity, would have to take his place with the main army in the field.

The Factions in the Austrian High Command

As Russia began pressing for a return to war with France, two factions formed in Austria. One, led by government foreign ministers Counts Cobenzl and Colloredo, believed an alliance with Russia was the only way to protect Austria from French ambitions. Opposed to them another faction, championed by Archduke Charles, the War Minister,

Archduke Charles opposed the war of 1805 and became immersed in a power struggle with FML Mack. Charles eventually commanded in northern Italy, fighting successfully at Caldiero before retreating due to events in Bavaria. (Heeresgeschichtliches Museum, Vienna)

Mack had been out of favour since 1799, but with powerful support behind him convinced Francis that he alone was capable of rapidly reforming and mobilising the army for a resumption of hostilities with France. (Heeresgeschichtliches Museum)

argued against war, believing the army was not yet suitably prepared for a renewal of hostilities. In addition, Charles felt a period of peace would allow Austria's economy and prosperity vital time to recover, before plunging into war again.

Charles, perceived as Austria's most able soldier, held a strong position, but his rival ministers worked against him, gaining the support of Francis. The war party then resurrected the career of Feldmarschalleutnant (FML) Mack, who had commanded the Neapolitan army in the 1799 campaign with disastrous results. Bringing him out of semi-retirement, they presented him as the expert who could really take hold of the army and shake it into a state of readiness, sooner rather than later. Mack told Francis exactly what he wanted to hear. He announced that he could have the army mobilised in a very short time and introduce tactical and logistic reforms that would place it on an equal footing with the French. When Francis compared this with Charles's consistently pessimistic (though realistic) view of the state of the army, he became convinced Mack was the man to turn around the army's fortunes. Francis began to authorise changes that weakened Charles's powerbase, while elevating Mack to chief of the Quartermaster General Staff. Charles continued voicing his opinions on the unprepared state of the army, and advocating northern Italy as the main theatre of future operations, with the forces destined to move through Bavaria held back until the Russians arrived. Meanwhile, Mack saw the move through Bavaria as the main thrust of any offensive. Francis considered the options, and Mack argued persuasively that Kutuzov's Russians would rendezvous with him in Bavaria five days before Napoleon could arrive. Convinced, Francis authorised Mack's advance towards the Bavarian capital, Munich, and to the Lech River beyond. To soothe Russian concerns about the status of the commander of this Austrian force, Francis appointed his brother-in-law, the young Archduke Ferdinand d'Este, as nominal commander in his absence. However, Ferdinand quickly discovered that Mack held full authority to override all his decisions. Against this backdrop of confusion and rivalry, Austria entered the war, with Mack leading the way. His benefactor, Count Cobenzl, expressed his delight with Mack's progress writing, ' ... what a difference one man can make in affairs when he is capable and understands his business.' However, by the time the three armies confronted each other at Austerlitz, FML Freiherr Karl Leiberich von Mack found himself relegated to the pages of history as 'the unfortunate Mack'.

Mikhail Illarionovich Golenishchev-Kutuzov

Born in 1745, Kutuzov had been destined for a military career right from the start. His father, a former military engineer, saw to it that his son enrolled in the Artillery-Engineer school at the age of 12. The young Kutuzov did well and emerged with the reputation of being a diligent and talented student. He saw action against the Poles in 1764 and against Turkey in 1768 when his bravery under fire earned him a reputation for courage. He proved talented and excelled in both staff work and field command. Four years later in the Crimea he was badly wounded in the head – the bullet entering 'between the eye and temple on one side of his face went out exactly the same spot on the other side'. Miraculously he recovered and following his return to duty, again in the Crimea, he served under the great Russian general Alexander Suvorov, who had a major influence on his thinking. War with the Turks broke out again in 1787 and Kutuzov, now commanding a Jäger corps at the siege of Ochakov, received another dangerous wound. The wound was in almost the same spot as his previous one and although it was at first thought fatal, he did recover, minus the sight of one eye. Kutuzov continued in the army, now with the rank of major-general, and despite his physical handicap continued to display bravery in battle that was second to none.

In 1793 the talented Kutuzov was despatched to Constantinople to act as Ambassador Extraordinary to Turkey, a service he performed with great success. A year later he returned to St. Petersburg where he was promoted to lieutenant-general and command of the army based in Finland. This was in addition to his appointment as Director of the Land Cadet Corps, entrusted with the training of future officers of the army. However, Russia had further need of Kutuzov's diplomatic skills, and when Tsar Paul I came to the throne he was despatched to Berlin, where he succeeded in strengthening the relationship between Russia and Prussia. Following the end of Paul's short reign Alexander installed Kutuzov as military governor of St. Petersburg and Infantry Inspector for Finland. However, in 1801 he was relieved of these responsibilities and went into retirement on his estate in the Ukraine.

The formation of the Third Coalition and the imminent war led to Kutuzov's recall. Now 60 years old, he had lost much of his earlier spirit and dash. He was portly and fond of life's comforts – particularly alcohol and women – but he was also cunning, shrewd, diplomatic and dogged. Although Alexander disliked him, his reputation and achievements were such that he was the obvious choice as commander-in-chief. He answered the call, disapproved of the Allied strategy, but following orders led his Russian army westwards. At the final confrontation at Austerlitz, the presence of Tsar Alexander seriously undermined his position as commander-in-chief.

The difference in the command structures of France and the Allies is clear to see. Napoleon bore supreme responsibility for all matters, both civil and military. True loyalty from officers and men alike, coupled with a genuine belief in his abilities on the field of battle, ensured his orders were executed without question, enabling him to respond quickly to changes or developments. For the Russians and Austrians, the position was far more complex. Internal dissension, intrigues, distrust, an over-ambitious plan and lack of a clear overall command structure meant they were at a disadvantage from the start.

Mikhail Kutuzov began his highly successful military career at a young age, while at the same time developing great diplomatic skills. In 1805 he came out of retirement to lead the Russian army. (Sammlung Alfred und Roland Umhey)

OPPOSING ARMIES

THE FRENCH ARMY

The French army that embarked on the campaign of 1805 was the most highly trained of any in the Revolutionary/Napoleonic era. The inevitable deterioration in relations between Britain and France, following the Peace of Amiens, saw the French army reassemble in preparation for an invasion of England. In the summer of 1803 Napoleon issued orders for the formation of vast military camps along the Channel coast with others based in the newly acquired territory of Hanover and one at Bayonne. These camps became the permanent home of the army for the next two years. The soldiers who inhabited them had been moulded by the Revolutionary Wars, but Napoleon had plans to change them and develop new ways of using French manpower. The victors of Arcola, Rivoli, Marengo and Hohenlinden returned to school. Each day infantry companies exercised themselves in the finer points of battalion drill, with regular opportunities for firing practice and brigade drill. Divisional drill in battle situations completed the training, with the whole process repeated constantly. The cavalry trained in a similar manner. This constant training and the allocation of regiments, based on the camps they occupied, to permanent brigade and divisional formations, and ultimately corps, developed a strong esprit de corps amongst the units.

The *corps d'armée* was introduced as the standard military formation by Napoleon as the army retrained. Although it was not a new idea, he did perfect it to such an extent that Austria, Prussia and Russia all later adopted the principle. A corps was an all arms force; an army in miniature, capable of holding its own in combat until support arrived, and because of this strength it could disperse while on the march but concentrate quickly for battle. By being able to disperse the elements of the corps it could advance more rapidly over a wider area, and more easily supply itself from local resources.

The strength of a corps could vary enormously dependant upon its purpose. Of the seven corps that advanced to the Rhine at the end of September 1805, the weakest was Augereau's VII Corps with just under 14,000 men and 24 guns, while the strongest was Soult's IV Corps of about 30,000 with 36 guns. A corps would comprise two or more infantry divisions, a light cavalry division (sometimes only a brigade) and artillery with supporting personnel. As part of Napoleon's reorganisation he also created a cavalry reserve. This mass concentration of heavy cavalry, commanded by Marshal Murat, grouped two heavy cavalry divisions of carabiniers and cuirassiers with four mounted divisions and one dismounted division of dragoons, with artillery support. The dismounted division clearly demonstrates the great shortage of horses at the outset

A French light infantryman of 1805. Men such as this moved into the vast English Channel camps in 1803, emerging at the start of the 1805 campaign as France's best-trained army of the period. (*Le Bivouac*, Rousselot – Sammlung Alfred und Roland Umhey)

of the 1805 campaign. Alongside his creation of the cavalry reserve, Napoleon also developed an artillery reserve.

In July 1804 Napoleon reorganised his Consular Guard as a small corps in its own right, and renamed it the Imperial Guard. Placed under the command of Marshal Bessières the guard mustered six battalions of infantry, 10½ squadrons of cavalry and 24 guns, in all about 7,000 men.

The organisation of line and light battalions was similar in that each consisted of nine companies; eight of fusiliers and one of grenadiers in the line (ligne) battalions and seven of chasseurs and one each of carabiniers and voltigeurs in the light (légère) infantry. Three weeks after the army commenced its march for the Rhine, Napoleon ordered a final change; each line battalion was to convert one of its fusilier companies to voltigeurs. The difficulty of implementing this on the march ensured that not all corps managed to effectively change their organisation before Austerlitz. At full strength both line and light battalions theoretically comprised 1,070 men, however, maintaining this level on campaign was impossible. After the march from the Channel coast to Moravia, via Vienna, and with numerous battles and skirmishes along the way, the average strength of a battalion in Soult's IV Corps at Austerlitz was 730 men.

After two years of intensive training the order finally came; England was no longer the objective. Turning their backs to the Channel, *La Grande Armée* headed eastwards; seven corps, the Cavalry and Artillery Reserve, and the Imperial Guard, some 180,000 men, embarked on a journey that would ultimately lead to one of Napoleonic France's greatest victories.

The French army's great shortage of horses at the outbreak of war in 1805 forced the creation of a division of dismounted dragoons led by Général de division Baraguey d'Hilliers. (Sammlung Alfred und Roland Umhey)

THE AUSTRIAN ARMY

Archduke Charles emerged from the campaign of 1800 with his reputation intact and appeared the obvious choice to carry out the much needed army reforms. Charles, at the head of the new War Ministry, turned his attention to the army's administration, groaning under the weight of its own bureaucracy. Having streamlined matters he authorized improvements in the training of junior officers and attempted to make service in the army more attractive for those subject to conscription. In an effort to prevent large numbers of these potential recruits 'disappearing', he amended the existing lifelong conscription to a reduced period of enlistment; ten years in the infantry, 12 years in the cavalry and 14 years in the artillery and other technical branches.

The Austrian treasury was at this time very weak, which hindered the training of the army. Regiments were widely distributed, many in fortresses in the eastern regions of the empire where expenses were less. Further financial savings emerged from the almost universal employment of the furlough system, whereby new recruits received their basic military training, then were sent home on unpaid leave until required. With as much as 40 per cent of a unit's strength dispersed in this way rapid mobilisation became impossible. Despite this, the ordinary Austrian soldier performed well at the large periodic training camps but their officers came in for much criticism. In fact some observers claimed these exercises were outdated, as a result of which Archduke Charles was criticised for wasting too much time and expenditure on administration and too little on preparing the army for war.

The introduction of other cost-cutting exercises resulted in the cavalry losing seven regiments and a new three-battalion *Tiroler Jäger Regiment* replacing the 15 short-lived light infantry battalions.

The advent of a new coalition, and ultimately a new war, changed everything. When talks opened with the Russians, Charles warned the Emperor that if war broke out Austria was likely to have to face France alone before the 'untrustworthy' Russians arrived, a fact that could have serious implications for an economy that was already stretched. At this point FML Mack had a critical influence on the preparations for war. As chief of the Quartermaster General Staff, Mack was now in a position of power, and in the spring and summer of 1805 he began to introduce a series of reforms in the army that contributed to the general confusion, occurring as they did on the eve of war. In the cavalry he reduced the strength of both light and heavy squadrons and in the infantry he recommended that the third line of infantry should be used to extend the line or operate as skirmishers to the front. However, his decision in June 1805 to alter the composition of the infantry regiments caused more confusion than any other change. At that time, an infantry regiment comprised three field battalions, each of six fusilier companies, a depot battalion of four companies and a grenadier division of two

In 1805 the Austrian artillery suffered greatly from an inadequate establishment. Due to lack of manpower it was necessary to draw labouring support from untrained infantry-man while there was also a lack of permanent horse teams and drivers.

companies, in total 24 companies. The grenadier companies were detached from the parent regiment in the field and formed into composite grenadier battalions. Mack's changes rearranged these 24 companies into four field battalions and one depot battalion, each of four fusilier companies, and a grenadier battalion of four companies. No longer operating independently of their regiments, these grenadier battalions combined the original two grenadier companies with two companies drawn from the regiment's original first battalion.

Mack instigated other changes too. He believed that one of the main reasons for recent French successes was the mobility of the army, while the ponderous supply columns of the Austrian army had always hindered rapid movement. At a stroke Mack decreed that the Austrian army would follow the French principle and live from the country they passed through. With no experience of supporting themselves in this way the Army suffered greatly from lack of food during the campaign.

Charles objected, considering the eve of war an inappropriate time to make such sweeping changes. He failed to overturn the decision, however, and the confusing exchange of companies within battalions left one exasperated officer reflecting as he marched off to war that the 'common soldiers no longer knew their officers and their officers did not know their men'.

THE RUSSIAN ARMY

Like the French and Austrian armies, the Russian army too had been through a period of change. When Paul I became Tsar in 1796 he had taken a backward step and modelled the army on the lines of that of his great idol, Frederick the Great of Prussia. However, Paul's reign was short-lived and with Alexander as the new Tsar the re-modernisation of the army began.

Russia conscripted the army from her vast pool of manpower. The almost medieval structure of Russian life, with downtrodden peasants, or serfs, tied to the nobility and landowners, provided the army with an almost inexhaustible supply of material to fill the ranks. Conscription rules allowed substitutes whereby unscrupulous landowners could replace the chosen man with another of his workers. This meant that it was often the laziest, weakest or most dishonest workers that went forward to the army. With service lasting 25 years, once a recruit marched away his family never expected to see him again.

The blind obedience a serf had learnt as part of his upbringing made him perfect for service in the Russian army. The strict, formal drill imposed on the Russians, including the straight-legged 'goose-step' march, often instilled with excessive physical punishment, ensured that the average soldier followed every order explicitly without question even in the most trying of circumstances. Much emphasis on the use of the bayonet permeated training, a weapon that seemed ideally suited to the Russian soldier, while musketry practice played a lesser role. Many considered the Russian musket unreliable due to the poor quality of the powder the country produced. The Russian infantryman was steady, reliable and obstinately brave but poorly led. Russian line infantry officers at this time were considered by many to be the worst in Europe; poorly trained, uneducated and lacking experience in manoeuvring their men.

In his changes Alexander reintroduced regimental names based on regionality, grouping regiments, purely for administration purposes, in 'Inspections' based on provinces. Like the Austrian army, the regiment was still the highest permanent organisation, limiting opportunities for officers to gain experience with larger formations. Groupings at brigade or divisional level were on an ad hoc basis and could alter during a campaign. Alexander also altered regimental composition so that all grenadier, musketeer and jäger regiments consisted of three battalions.

There is some confusion regarding the uniform of Russian musketeers in 1805. The headwear of the army was going through a period of change from 1803, with the old bicorn being phased out. New shakos, first introduced in August 1803, had given way to a second version authorised in February 1805. However, authorised changes rarely mean instant adoption and it is possible that both bicorn and shako were worn by the musketeers in the field at Austerlitz. It is interesting to note, however, that it is generally accepted that cuirassier and dragoon regiments, also authorised to change from bicorns to helmets in 1803, had done so prior to the start of the campaign.

The cavalry recruited in much the same way as the infantry, merely creaming off those serfs with any basic familiarity with horses. However, in 1803 the need for economy in the army led Alexander to authorise the conversion of seven regiments of expensive cuirassiers to dragoons. Irregular Cossack cavalry supported the line cavalry.

Under Alexander, the Russian army experienced a period of reorganisation, but, once levied, conscripts still faced 25 years' service. Uniforms also developed as bicorns were phased out in the infantry and replaced with shakos. (Sammlung Alfred und Roland Umhey)

Russian officers wearing their winter uniforms. The Russian officer class was held in low esteem by contemporary observers, who considered them uneducated and poorly trained. (Philip Haythornthwaite)

The *Chevalier Garde,* the most
prestigious regiment in the
Russian army, formed part of the
Imperial Guard cavalry. It drew
its manpower from the upper
echelons of society.
(2 Décembre 1805, Jack Girbal –
Sammlung Alfred und Roland
Umhey)

The artillery had begun a series of reforms in 1801. The weight of
the barrels as well as the gun carriages and caissons were lightened,
following the example of France's Gribeauval system, but the new guns
lacked the hitting power of the French pieces.

When Kutuzov's army, some 46,000 strong, set out on 25 August 1805
it had a long, gruelling westward march ahead of it. In order to get
under way at all they were heavily reliant on the Austrian army to supply
them with many of their basic requirements. To ensure the Russians
kept moving Austria also supplied staff officers, a skilled role that
was largely lacking in the Russian army. These weaknesses in supply,
equipment and leadership contributed to the rapid deterioration of
Kutuzov's command. Three months after it marched for Bavaria,
Kutuzov's army had already been forced to fall back to Moravia. Having
marched almost 900 miles and fought a series of rearguard actions, his
command now numbered only about half its original strength.

OPENING MOVES

ADVANCE TO THE DANUBE

Having determined to turn his army away from England and prepare for battle with Austria and Russia, Napoleon wasted no time in issuing new orders for a concentration of the army on the Rhine. On 26 August 1805 Bernadotte's I Corps marched from Hanover towards Frankfurt while Marmont's II Corps left Holland marching for Mainz. The rest of the army departed its coastal cantonments and moved towards positions between Mainz and Strasbourg. At this point Napoleon knew little of the Allies' plan of campaign, but he anticipated intercepting them somewhere between the Lech and Inn Rivers in Bavaria.

Some 750 miles away, far to the east of the Rhine, Kutuzov set out from Russian territory on 25 August and marched his ponderous army across Austrian Galicia towards the border with Moravia, which he reached on 22 September. He was still some 265 miles short of his initial target, Braunau, on the Inn River. Meanwhile, *La Grande Armée* was already concentrating along the line of the Rhine, and launched its advance across the river on 25 September.

The Austrian army of FML Mack was also on the move. The leading elements of the army left Wels on 5 September and crossed the Inn River into Bavaria three days later. Having anticipated the 22,000 men of the Bavarian army joining him, Mack must have been dismayed to find that

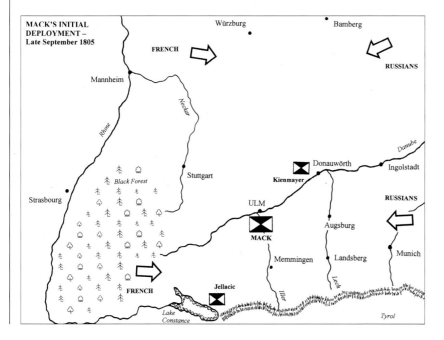

Mack anticipated that the French would advance in two main thrusts and positioned his main force to intercept them on the Iller River, believing that the Russians would be in a position to be able to oppose any French move further to the north.

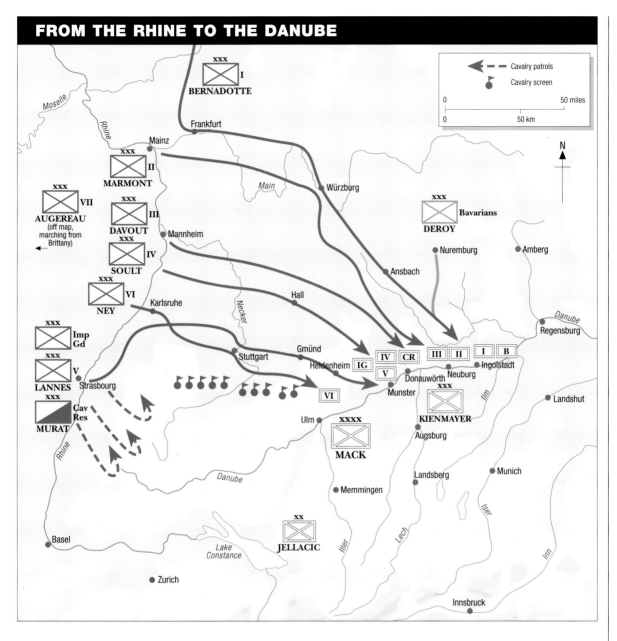

Bavaria was now allied to France. Mack had intended holding a position on the Lech while waiting for the Russians, however, hearing news that the French were already on the Rhine he pushed forward. He chose a new position further west on the Iller River, between Ulm and Memmingen, from where he could oppose any French attempt to exit the Black Forest. Archduke Ferdinand, the nominal commander of the army, objected to the forward deployment but Mack refused to listen. Emperor Francis, arriving at the front, approved Mack's dispositions and departed again. Such was the bitterness between Ferdinand and Mack that they rarely spoke again, preferring to communicate in writing.

It was Mack's opinion that the French would advance in two bodies. He anticipated one thrust on the Iller and the other further north, pushing towards Würzburg, where he believed it would encounter the

ABOVE **Marshal Bernadotte, marching from Hanover, led his I Corps and Marmont's II Corps through the neutral Prussian territory of Ansbach. This advance took Mack by surprise as he received assurances that Prussia would oppose any such move.**

RIGHT **The French army marching for the Danube. The weather in October 1805 was atrocious and the men suffered greatly; they in turn inflicted much hardship on the Bavarian villages they passed through. (Girbal – Sammlung Alfred und Roland Umhey)**

Russians advancing in support. To face this threat he had a simple plan. With his main force in position around the Iller and flanking forces close to Lake Constance covering the Tyrol (FML Jellacic), and on the Danube watching the north (FML Kienmayer), he felt secure. Prussia's declaration that they would defend their neutrality removed any threat to his rear through the territory of Ansbach and added to his feeling of security. With his rear secure he would be able to swing his force to face a threat from his front or right without compromising a line of retreat, holding the French while the Russians moved up in support.

On 17 September Napoleon learned that the Austrian army had pushed forward to Ulm and the Iller River. His original plan had been for his army to converge on the Danube between Ulm and Donauwörth, but now, with this information he ordered a concentration slightly further to the east, between Günzburg and Ingolstädt. The great sweeping advance of the French army was not as smooth as some accounts of the campaign would have us believe. Murat's cavalry, crossing the Rhine at Strasbourg, were to push through the Black Forest and occupy Austrian advance troops, thus shielding the movements of the army, but most importantly, take prisoners to gather information on Austrian intentions. In this final task they failed. There was also friction between the corps commanders and Berthier, the chief-of-staff, who at times issued contradictory orders. The advance also suffered greatly from the weather. If the opposing generals had been anticipating

pleasant autumnal weather they were to be disappointed. October was a month of incessant wind, rain, sleet and snow. The roads disintegrated under the march of such a mass of men, and food was in short supply. The Bavarian inhabitants, France's new allies, who found themselves in the path of Napoleon's marauding army suffered greatly as cold, tired and hungry soldiers helped themselves to whatever they wanted.

Although he did not yet know it, Mack was already in serious trouble. Late in September Murat (Cavalry Reserve), Lannes (V Corps) and the Imperial Guard had crossed the Rhine at Strasbourg. About 35 miles downstream Ney's VI Corps also crossed, while further down the river Soult's IV Corps and Davout's III Corps commenced their south-eastward move. Furthest north, Bernadotte's I Corps crossed the Main River at Frankfurt, closely accompanied by Marmont's II Corps, which passed the Rhine at Mainz. These two corps were heading for Würzburg. Bernadotte, with overall command of this force and the Bavarians, was already in receipt of orders to march through Ansbach, defying the Prussians whose territory it was. Despite their assurances to the Allies, Prussia did nothing to oppose this move.

On 4 October Mack received information that convinced him that the French push through the Black Forest was a feint and that the main French army was moving north of the Danube. To face this threat he ordered a concentration of the army along the Danube from Ulm extending towards Donauwörth. Then on 5 October he received news that French troops were approaching through Ansbach. Napoleon also received information about this time of Mack concentrating his forces

Napoleon at Augsburg on the Lech river with men of Marmont's II Corps. Having crossed the Danube Napoleon set up his headquarters in the city while Bernadotte secured Munich and Soult occupied Landsberg. (Musée national du château de Versailles – Sammlung Alfred und Roland Umhey)

on Ulm. On 7 October Soult and Murat began to cross the Danube at Donauwörth. Kienmayer, the Austrian right flank guard, fell back southwards to ensure communications with Ulm could be maintained.

Mack considered his options but felt no major change was necessary. He was determined to maintain his position west of the Lech River, to await the Russians. He reasoned any withdrawal to the east would abandon the Tyrol to the French and a retreat towards the Tyrol would have exposed Kutuzov to the full weight of the French army.

NAPOLEON CROSSES THE DANUBE

On 8 October Lannes, Davout, Marmont and Bernadotte began crossing the Danube while Murat's cavalry and Lannes' infantry combined to overwhelm an Austrian advance guard marching towards the Lech at Wertingen. The battle gave Napoleon the prisoners he so desired. He was now sure that Mack was still holding Ulm and he had a good idea of his strength. Napoleon considered Mack's most likely escape routes would be to the east via Augsburg or south to the Tyrol. Accordingly he ordered Augsburg, Landsberg and Memmingen occupied. However, these dispositions had left an opening for Mack. With almost all of the French army south of the Danube preparing for an Austrian movement east or south, only two divisions remained north of the river and one of those was about to be ordered south. Mack did not know just how weak the French were but intended to attack their communications. On 11 October the Austrian army, less one brigade left to hold Ulm, crossed to the north bank of the Danube from where it observed Dupont's

Marshall Ney orders his men across the bridge at Elchingen on 14 October. This timely attack prevented an attempted breakout from Ulm by the garrison despite a number of brilliant charges by the Austrian cavalry. (Stadtarchiv Ulm – Sammlung Alfred und Roland Umhey)

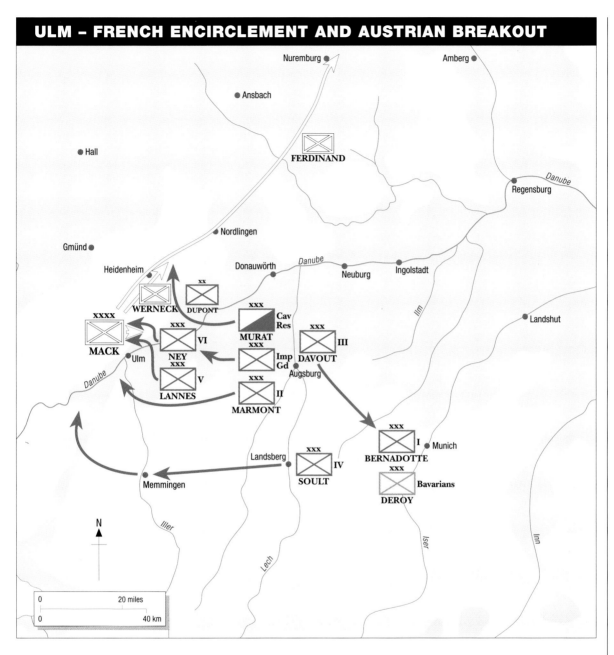

unsupported division of VI Corps at Haslach. The Austrians heavily outnumbered the French but it was only after a long, bloody struggle, that the poorly co-ordinated Austrian attack eventually forced Dupont to withdraw. The Austrians returned to their positions at Ulm but Mack's complex plans to exploit the French weakness faced strong opposition from some of his commanders, leading to a postponement until 13 October. On that day Mack planned a breakout, but that too was disrupted as he insisted on rearranging the composition of the columns. Two columns, perhaps totalling 35,000 men, were to advance north of the Danube towards Elchingen to clear the way, with two more columns bringing up the rear. Brushing Dupont aside, they would make for Bohemia and unite with the Russians.

The report of the action at Haslach alerted Napoleon to the confusion that existed in VI Corps and to Dupont's isolated position. In response he ordered Ney to secure the river crossing at Elchingen by the morning of 14 October. The last remaining escape route from the trap was about to be cut.

Having set the move to Elchingen in motion, Mack began to ponder new information that was coming in. What he found confusing was that French troops were moving towards Ulm and the Iller, south of the Danube. If Napoleon wanted to attack the city of Ulm, which lay on the north bank of the river, why would he approach from the south? Then on the morning of 13 October he received an unofficial report that claimed a British force had landed at Boulogne and that a revolution had broken out in France. Everything was clear to him now – Napoleon was retreating to the Rhine and doing so on the 'safe' side of the Danube. The orders for the columns detailed to follow up the breakout attempt on the north bank were countermanded; these troops would now be required to pursue the 'retreating' French to the south. It was only later that Mack discovered that the infamous spy Charles Schulmeister had duped him. The confusion did not end there. On the morning of 14 October one of Mack's columns fell back on Ulm, having been intercepted by the French at Elchingen. Meanwhile the second column under FML Werneck, with the Reserve Artillery, unaware of events at Elchingen continued to push on unsupported.

THE SURRENDER OF ULM

Back in Ulm all was gloom and despondency. The myth that the French were retreating had been shattered and there now appeared little likelihood of escape. Mack argued with his officers and his on-going

The capitulation of Ulm. Surrounded by the French army and with no sign of Russian intervention, Mack surrendered on 20 October. Some 25,000 Austrians marched from the city into captivity. (Versailles – Sammlung Alfred und Roland Umhey)

feud with Archduke Ferdinand boiled over. He felt sure that by defending the city they could tie down a large French force until the Russians arrived. Ferdinand had had enough. He was not going to endure capture by the French. Having confronted Mack one last time, Ferdinand, supported by FML Schwarzenberg, gathered 12 squadrons of cavalry and abandoned Ulm that night, hoping to link up with FML Werneck's column of 20,000 men.

On 15 October the French completed the encirclement of Ulm and began an artillery bombardment of the walls, summoning the city to surrender. Mack rejected their demand – he had approximately 23,000 men still under command and was determined to tie down the French, but the clock was ticking. Meanwhile the first exhausted units of Kutuzov's Russian army had begun to arrive in Braunau on the Bavarian border about 160 miles away, but it would be another two weeks before they regrouped and were ready for action. By then it was all over.

Mack received another summons to surrender on 17 October. In his growing desperation he agreed to surrender his army as prisoners of war on 25 October if at that time there was no sign of Russian intervention. Austrian morale in the city was shattered. The weather continued its assault on body and mind, and limited French infiltration into the city as part of the agreement made matters worse. On 19 October Napoleon met with Mack and informed him that Werneck's column had surrendered. With a written guarantee from Berthier that the Russians could not arrive in the area in time, Mack signed the surrender. The following afternoon an Austrian army of 51 battalions, 18¼ squadrons and 67 guns marched out of Ulm into captivity. It was 20 October; the following day Admiral Lord Nelson's British fleet destroyed the combined fleets of France and Spain at Trafalgar.

All that remained of the Austrian army that had marched into Bavaria some 72,000 strong was Kienmayer's column and the mounted men that Archduke Ferdinand had brought out of Ulm, boosted by cavalry from Werneck's column that had escaped capture. These joined Kutuzov at Braunau. Jellacic's column failed to escape into the Tyrol and surrendered to Augereau's VII Corps after its long march from Brittany. The first Kutuzov knew of the capitulation at Ulm was when Mack, on parole, rode into Braunau, on his way to Vienna and eventual court-martial.

In northern Italy Archduke Charles had undertaken his task with little enthusiasm. He was convinced Mack would lead his army to disaster. Accordingly he chose to stand on the defensive, with Vienna's approval, and not push into Lombardy until the situation in Bavaria was clarified. On 17 October Masséna, commanding the French forces, commenced his advance, encouraging Charles to fall back on a prepared position at Caldiero. Here, on 24 October, he received news of Mack's surrender and determined to oppose Masséna, defeat him, and thus gain time to withdraw on Austria. The two sides clashed over three days at the end of October, eventually Masséna fell back allowing Charles to commence his retirement. The grand strategy of the Third Alliance was in tatters.

THE ALLIES RETREAT

At Braunau Kutuzov considered his options. Ultimately his choice was

On 13 November Marshal Murat captured the vital bridge over the Danube in Vienna by a mixture of bluff and bravado. He then marched north and made contact with the retreating Russians but was himself duped, allowing the main body to escape. (Philip Haythornthwaite)

simple; he had no intention of risking his depleted force of 27,000 men against a victorious French army. Having finally reassembled his men it was time to turn around and retreat back the way he had come. Accordingly on 25 October he set out for Wels with the French in pursuit. Napoleon had to consider this move carefully. By pushing up the Danube valley towards Vienna, he extended his lines of communication at a time when it appeared Prussia was finally shaking off its lethargy in response to Bernadotte's violation of Ansbach. Napoleon decided to take a bold course and push on quickly in an attempt to crush Kutuzov before he received reinforcements. Kutuzov handled the retreat well, fighting rearguard actions at Ried, Lambach and Amstetten. An increasingly worried Austrian Emperor urged Kutuzov to defend Vienna by making a stand at St. Pölten. However, Kutuzov had no intention of risking his army to protect the Austrian capital and crossed to the north bank of the Danube at Krems, the last crossing before Vienna, burning the bridge behind him. Safe from immediate pursuit Kutuzov decided to turn the tables on the French and attacked the newly created VIII Corps. Under Mortier it had crossed to the north of the Danube at Linz and was now isolated from the rest of the army. The clash that followed at Dürnstein on 11 November saw Mortier's men extricate themselves from the Russian trap but only after a fiercely contested battle. Kutuzov planned to maintain his position at Krems to await Buxhöwden, but the following day Murat entered Vienna and on 13 November, by an extraordinary display of bluff and possible collusion, captured the main bridge over the Danube. With his position compromised Kutuzov recommenced his retreat.

As soon as the Vienna bridge was in French hands Napoleon ordered a rapid pursuit of Kutuzov, hoping to intercept him around Znaim on the road to Brünn. Murat made contact with a Russian flank guard at Schöngrabern, but in attempting to delay them by entering into negotiations he was double-bluffed by Kutuzov. The wily Russian sent two ADCs to discuss terms for an armistice. Completely taken-in, Murat sent details of the armistice to Napoleon for verification, while the main body of the Russians continued their retreat screened by this flank guard. Napoleon was furious when he heard, and he ordered Murat to attack. The Russian flank guard, commanded by Bagration, fought doggedly against overwhelming numbers and despite heavy casualties extricated themselves and rejoined Kutuzov two days later. Napoleon's pursuit of Kutuzov had failed. Between 17 November and 25 November the great concentration of the Allied army took place at Olmütz in Moravia. Here Buxhöwden's army, the Russian Imperial Guard and the Austrian Prince Johann von Liechtenstein joined Kutuzov. Liechtenstein now commanded Kienmayer's men, as well as other troops that had been in the vicinity of Vienna. Resplendent amongst this great multinational gathering of mud-splattered and tattered soldiery stood their Imperial Majesties, Tsar and Kaiser, the Emperors of Russia and Austria. To Alexander and his arrogantly over-confident entourage, the widely dispersed French army, at the end of an extended line of communication, appeared very vulnerable.

THE MARCH TO AUSTERLITZ

Napoleon halted his pursuit of the Russians at Brünn on 20 November. Marshal Soult pushed IV Corps forward towards Austerlitz, where at the great battle of 2 December he was to play a pivotal role. (Philip Haythornthwaite)

Prince Dolgoruki, one of the young, over-confident and vociferous ADCs who had great influence on the Tsar's thinking. (Hulton Getty)

THE EAGLES GATHER

Napoleon halted the pursuit of the Russians at Brünn on 20 November. This was a vital respite for the exhausted and hungry army and allowed time for rest and for the vast tail of stragglers to be rounded up. Only four formations lay close by, the Imperial Guard and Lannes V Corps were around the city while Murat's Cavalry Reserve and Soult's IV Corps were positioned to the east of it. Bernadotte, with his I Corps and a division of Bavarians, was some 50 miles north-west of Brünn, watching for any movement by Archduke Ferdinand from Prague. Marmont's II Corps in Styria, about 80 miles south-west of Vienna, could oppose Archduke Charles should he attempt to march on the Austrian capital. East of Vienna, Davout held III Corps ready to counter any hostile movement from Hungary while Mortier's mauled VIII Corps garrisoned the city. After Ulm, Marshal Ney marched to the Tyrol and Augereau's VII Corps provided a number of garrisons along the line of communications. The apparent weakness of the French army around Brünn, however, was misleading. By means of forced marches Napoleon felt sure he could rapidly add the corps of Bernadotte and Davout to his main force. Like the Russians, Napoleon too sought a battle, sooner rather than later, as reports that the Prussian army had commenced mobilisation were beginning to reach him. His supposed weakness now worked in his favour.

On 20 November the French and Russian cavalry clashed beyond Brünn at Raussnitz. The French drove the Russians off but the repercussions were to be great. Two of Alexander's ADCs, Prince Dolgoruki, one of the most vociferous and arrogant, and Wintzingerode, were elated, convincing the Tsar that with his Imperial Majesty at its head the army could defeat Napoleon in a major battle. It was what Alexander wanted to hear.

The following day Soult's Corps pushed beyond the large village of Austerlitz while an advanced cavalry brigade occupied Wischau, about halfway between Brünn and the Allied army. Napoleon rode out behind these forward posts and observed the ground closely. On the return journey from Wischau he stopped on the road close to a small hill between the village of Bellowitz and the post house at Posorsitz. Turning to the south he observed the ground carefully. It seemed clear to him that this was the most suitable terrain he had seen on which to fight the Allied army. Situated about four miles west of Austerlitz, a high plateau above the village of Pratze dominated the area. To the west of this plateau the ground sloped gently down to the wide valley of the Goldbach stream, along which were strung a series of small villages. Returning to Brünn, Murat and Lannes received orders to prepare their commands for an eastward redeployment.

On 24 November Alexander called a Council of War at Olmütz. The Allies had a number of options open to them. They could maintain their positions and await the army of Archduke Charles, who was retreating from Italy via Hungary and had already united with Archduke John's army from the Tyrol. Alternatively they could either move into Hungary, effecting an earlier junction with Charles, or continue to retire eastwards, drawing the French after them. A final option would be to advance and engage Napoleon. Reports on the state of supplies in the area made bleak reading. If the army stayed there much longer it would starve. Kutuzov advocated a further retirement to fresh supplies; any French pursuit would find the countryside stripped bare. A number of senior generals supported the commander-in-chief, but in reality he was no longer in command. With Alexander present, Kutuzov commanded in name only. The Tsar's circle of belligerent staff officers urged that the army attack, defeat Napoleon and bring glory to Russia. No one on the Russian side really cared what the Austrians thought anymore. Since the surrender at Ulm friction had grown between the two allies. The Russians now had a low opinion of the fighting capabilities of their Austrian allies and the continual objections to Russian excesses against the civilian population irked them. However, there was still one Austrian who had the ear of the Tsar, Generalmajor Weyrother, Kutuzov's replacement chief-of-staff. Following the death of FML Schmidt, at Dürnstein, Kutuzov appointed Weyrother to replace him. Weyrother has been described as possessing great personal courage but lacking confidence in voicing his own considered opinions or in offering contentious advice. He did, however, add the weight of his support for an attack towards Brünn. Alexander listened to the arguments but it was clear he wanted to face Napoleon on the field of battle. Kutuzov felt unable to oppose the wishes of the Tsar and stepped back. Emperor Francis, demoralised and a fugitive from his own capital, declined to offer any opposition. Alexander and his advisors confidently formulated their strategy the following day, 25 November, with the intention that the Allied army would commence its advance. In essence the plan was designed to turn the French right at Brünn, threaten their communications with Vienna and drive them back through difficult country towards Krems on the Danube. However, administrative delays meant it was not until the morning of 27 November that the 73,000 men of the Austro-Russian army launched their offensive. It was only the following day that Napoleon heard of the advance, effectively shielded as it was by the Allied advance guard under Bagration. Napoleon had deliberately not pressed the Allies, hoping to create an impression of weakness that might encourage them to consider battle. Now he had the news he wanted.

THE ALLIES ADVANCE

On the morning of 28 November the Russians pressed forward against the village of Wischau, held by a brigade of Murat's cavalry. The village was taken, the news of which prompted Napoleon to send one of his trusted aides, General Savary, to Allied headquarters to seek information, under the pretext of peace discussions. Savary reported back on the lack of unity amongst the officers and that the Tsar's

The French army begins to strengthen the defences on the hill on which Napoleon anchored the northern end of his line at Austerlitz. The hill, known to the French as the Santon, was fortified with captured Austrian guns. (Versailles – Sammlung Alfred und Roland Umhey)

influential entourage was encouraging him to seek battle. Napoleon determined to send Savary back with a request for a meeting with the Tsar in order to keep up the pretence that he was not in a position to accept battle. Then, turning his attention to the army, he began to issue a flurry of orders. The next day, 29 November, Soult (IV Corps), east of Austerlitz, and Murat (Cavalry Reserve), west of Raussnitz, were to abandon their current positions and withdraw westwards to the position he had selected behind the Goldbach stream, abandoning the dominating Pratzen plateau in the process. Lannes' V Corps and the Imperial Guard also received orders to take up positions behind the Goldbach. Bernadotte, who was some 50 miles away, close to the Bohemian border, was to march at once with I Corps, leaving the Bavarian division to watch for Archduke Ferdinand. Davout's III Corps, spread out between Vienna and Pressburg (Bratislava), were ordered to commence the long march north. Napoleon would thus gather an army of 74,500 men.

While the French were moving to their new positions the Allies spent 29 November redeploying their army, currently concentrated against the French left. This was not completed until the following day. Savary returned to the French lines, not with the Tsar, but with Prince Dolgoruki. The Russian prince and other influential officers interpreted the apparent French withdrawal as a sign of weakness. The Tsar's overconfident ADC bombarded Napoleon with demands, which he listened to with increasing anger before finally dismissing the Russian aristocrat, having made sure he had observed only what Napoleon wanted him to see. Dolgoruki returned to confirm the French were withdrawing and only cavalry patrols remained on the dominating Pratzen plateau.

Later on 30 November Napoleon led the Corps commanders across the area that would soon become the battlefield. Starting at the northern extreme, the left of the French line, they examined the hill by the Brünn–Olmütz road by which Napoleon had stopped on 21 November. Named the Santon by its defenders, efforts to make the hill more

The 49-year-old Lieutenant-General Dokhturov, commander of I Column of the Allied army at Austerlitz. Together with I Column's Advance Guard under Kienmayer he formed on the extreme left of the army.

defensible were successful and a number of captured Austrian artillery pieces enhanced its firepower. From here Napoleon and his entourage rode up on to the Pratzen plateau and observed off to the east the Austro-Russian army manoeuvring into position. Here Napoleon expanded on his plan of battle to his heedful audience, explaining that by abandoning the high ground he hoped to draw the Allies into a major battle. Later that evening Napoleon received news that Bernadotte and I Corps were at Brünn, and Davout himself arrived ahead of his men, who were suffering greatly on their forced march. Davout informed Napoleon that he anticipated that only the leading elements of III Corps, Friant's infantry division and Bourcier's dragoon division would arrive in time for battle.

THE ARMIES PREPARE FOR BATTLE

On 1 December the Allied army, disordered during its redeployment to the south, received new column identification numbers. At the start of the advance from Olmütz the army had marched with an advance guard and five columns, numbered one to five, starting from the right of the line. Now the columns numbered one to five from the left of the line. The confusion amongst the staff, attempting to issue orders for the advance towards the Pratzen plateau, must have been great. Despite these distractions the Austro-Russian army finally took up its position late on 1 December. On the left was Lieutenant-General Dokhturov in command of I Column, which formed camp on the Pratzen plateau above the village of Klein Hostieradek with a battalion of Jäger pushed

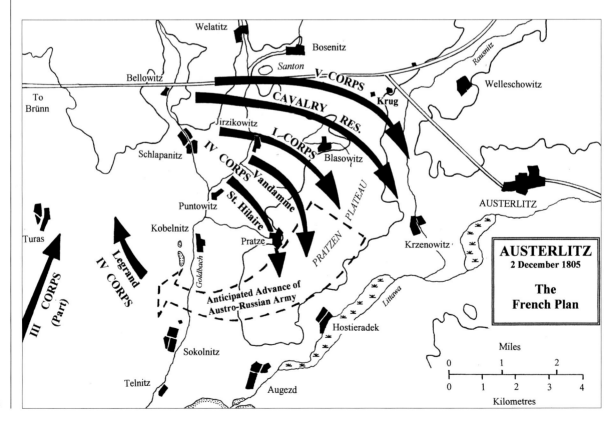

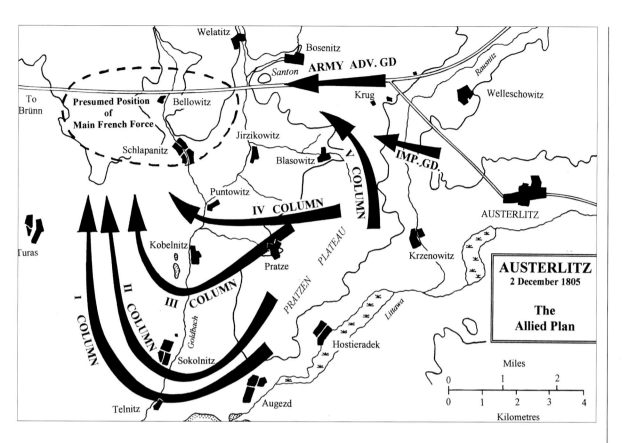

The map shows:

Welatitz — Bosenitz — ARMY ADV. GD — *Santon* — Krug — Welleschowitz — *Rausnitz*

To Brünn — **Presumed Position of Main French Force** — Bellowitz — Jirzikowitz — V COLUMN — IMP. GD.

Schlapanitz — Blasowitz — AUSTERLITZ

Puntowitz — IV COLUMN — Krzenowitz

Turas — Kobelnitz — PRATZEN PLATEAU

Pratze — I COLUMN — II COLUMN — III COLUMN — *Goldbach* — *Littawa*

AUSTERLITZ
2 December 1805

The Allied Plan

Hostieradek

Sokolnitz

Miles
0   1   2
0   1   2   3   4
Kilometres

Telnitz — Augezd

The Allied plan acknowledged the weakness of the French right and was designed to allow four columns to sweep round and drive it back on its main body when, with the added weight of the rest of the army, the French would be driven off.

LEFT Napoleon's plan depended on convincing the Allies of the weakness of his own right. Once the Allies were committed he anticipated that Davout would arrived, aiding weight to the right while Soult unleashed IV Corps against the Allies' now weakened centre.

forward to the village of Augezd at the southern foot of the plateau. Kienmayer's Advance Guard of I Column, encamped to the west of Augezd. To the right of I Column Lieutenant-General Langeron formed II Column. Lieutenant-General Prebyshevsky had marched towards Pratze and halted III Column on the plateau above and to the right of the village. These three columns, mainly Russian in composition, came under the overall command of Lieutenant-General Buxhöwden. IV Column, formed of Russian and Austrian troops under the joint command of Lieutenant-General Miloradovich and Feldzeugmeister Kolowrat, took up a position on the plateau to the rear of III Column. The main cavalry force, V Column, under Feldmarschalleutant Johann Liechtenstein followed behind III and IV Columns and were to make camp below the plateau. Bagration's Advance Guard was in position to the north, across the Brünn–Olmütz road, reaching towards the Pratzen plateau. In reserve Grand Prince Constantine held the Russian Imperial Guard on the high ground between Austerlitz and the Allied headquarters at Krzenowitz. With the left protected by a series of shallow ice-covered ponds towards the villages of Satschan and Menitz, the centre on the dominating Pratzen plateau and the right refused, the position was strong defensively. Unfortunately for the soldiers of the Allied army the Tsar was not intending to wage a defensive battle.

With the advance of the Austro-Russian army the French cavalry outposts had withdrawn to their own lines. Napoleon had his army heavily concentrated on their left, presenting a weak right to the Allies. Napoleon hoped to draw the Allies on to his right, then, with Davout arriving from the south in strength he would unleash his left against the

The Allied commanders discuss Weyrother's battle plan at headquarters in Krzenowitz during the night of 1/2 December. The assembled officers greeted the plans with little enthusiasm. (Sammlung Alfred und Roland Umhey)

Allies' right and rear. It was now clear, however, that Davout would not be able to bring the full weight of his corps to bear. In addition, news came in that suggested the Allies were massing their strength further to the south than he had anticipated. To combat this Napoleon ordered Davout to march for Turas, to the west of the line of the Goldbach to oppose any Allied push that reached this far. Soult's IV Corps was to make the decisive move, an oblique attack on the Pratzen plateau once the Allies were moving against the right, and drive a wedge between the two wings of the army. Murat's cavalry was to operate between Soult and Lannes' V Corps. In readiness behind Lannes was Oudinot's Grenadier Division and Bernadotte's I Corps. In reserve, the Imperial Guard stood close to Napoleon's headquarters on Zuran hill. Having completed these dispositions the sudden sound of firing far off to the south disturbed Napoleon. Despatching staff to find out what was happening, he was eventually informed at about midnight that the Austrians had attacked the village of Telnitz and driven off the defenders. Napoleon rode out to see for himself and was almost captured by a patrol of cossacks who chased him and his party back over the Goldbach. Napoleon returned to his headquarters through the bivouacs of the army. As he passed through the lines of soldiers they spontaneously held burning torches aloft to illuminate his progress and in the process caused the Allies to believe the French were about to launch a torchlight attack. However,

the move against Telnitz caused Napoleon to reconsider his positions
once more. Although a regiment of Legrand's division of IV Corps had
recaptured Telnitz, Napoleon deployed the remaining elements of the
division along the Goldbach to defend the villages of Sokolnitz and
Kobelnitz. This denied Lannes his support, as Bernadotte moved to the
right to back up the spearhead of IV Corps, forming behind Vandamme,
while the Reserve Grenadiers joined the Imperial Guard as army
reserve. These were the final dispositions before battle commenced.

During the day of 1 December Weyrother had been devising his battle
plan. The Allies still did not have a great amount of information about the
French dispositions, but movement on the Brünn–Olmütz road, the
strengthening of the Santon hill and a lack of troops along the Goldbach
in the Telnitz-Sokolnitz-Kobelnitz area suggested a concentration on
the left. These positions gave birth to a plan that demanded a vast, well
co-ordinated sweep by the Allied left and centre that would drive the
presumed weak French right back on its centre and left. Then, with the
added weight of the Advance Guard and cavalry of V Column, supported

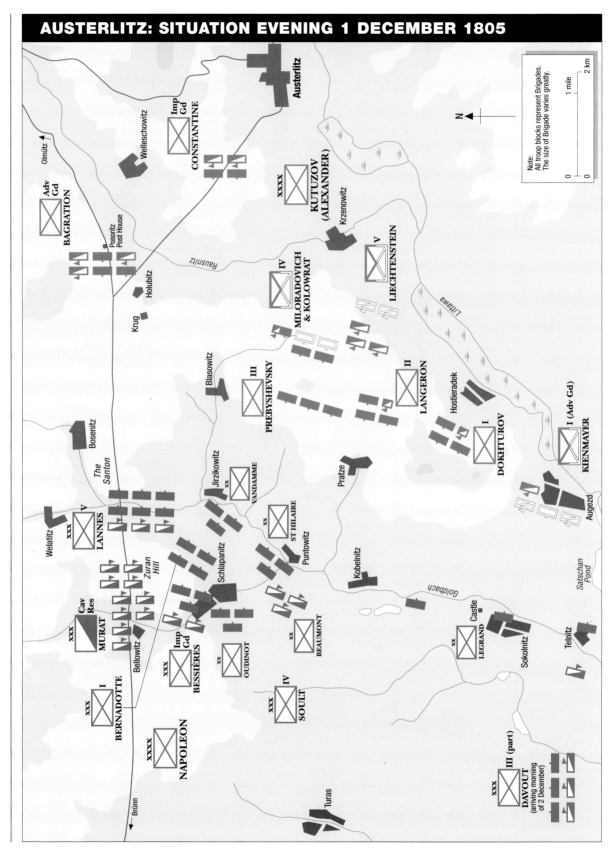

Note:
All troop blocks represent Brigades.
The size of Brigade varies greatly.

N

0
0
1 mile
2 km

Austerlitz

Welleschowitz

Imp
Gd
CONSTANTINE

Olmütz

Adv
Gd
BAGRATION

KUTUZOV
(ALEXANDER)

Krzenowitz

Posoritz
Post House

Rausnitz

Holubitz

Krug

IV
MILORADOVICH
& KOLOWRAT

V
LIECHTENSTEIN

Littawa

Blasowitz

III
PREBYSHEVSKY

II
LANGERON

Hostieradek

I (Adv Gd)
KIENMAYER

Bosenitz

The Santon

Jirzikowitz

xx
VANDAMME

I
DOKHTUROV

Welatitz

V
LANNES

xxx

Zuran
Hill

Schlapanitz

Pratze

xx
ST HILAIRE

Puntowitz

Kobelnitz

Goldbach

Satschan
Pond

Cav
Res

xxx
MURAT

Bellowitz

Imp
Gd

xxx
BESSIÈRES

xx
OUDINOT

xx
BEAUMONT

Castle

xx
LEGRAND

Sokolnitz

Telnitz

I

xxx
BERNADOTTE

IV

xxx
SOULT

XXXX
NAPOLEON

Brünn

Turas

III (part)

xxx
DAVOUT
(arriving morning
of 2 December)

by the Russian Imperial Guard, the French would be forced north, off their line of communications, or back on Brünn. At about midnight on 1 December the Allied column commanders gathered at headquarters in Krzenowitz where Weyrother lectured the assembled officers on their roles in the coming battle. It appears that those who were to carry out his plans were unimpressed. According to Langeron, commander of II Column, Kutuzov was 'half-asleep in a chair when we arrived at his house, and by the time we came to leave he had dozed off completely. Buxhöwden [overall commander of I, II and III Columns] was standing. He listened to what was being said, though it must have gone in one ear and out the other. Miloradovich [joint commander of IV Column] spoke not a word. Prebyshevsky [commander III Column] kept in the background, and only Dokhturov [commander I Column] examined the map with any attention.' Neither Alexander nor Francis was present. The advance by Buxhöwden's left wing, timed to commence at 7.00am in the morning was to be preceded by an advance guard of I Column, under the Austrian FML Kienmayer, who would clear Telnitz of its defenders. The plan was clear evidence of the view amongst the Russian hierarchy that the French were weak and intent on avoiding battle. With little resistance anticipated on the Goldbach to hinder the great sweep of the army Weyrother felt it unnecessary to allocate a reserve on the left. With no French counter-attack contemplated the plan required that all units descend from the security of the Pratzen plateau to ensure the French would not escape. The only reserve, the imposing formation of the Russian Imperial Guard, stood towards the right of centre but too far away to influence matters elsewhere on the battlefield. Desperate staff officers spent the rest of the night attempting to distribute written orders.

The night of 1/2 December had been freezing and the soldiers of the Austro-Russian army spent it huddled around their meagre campfires until roused, while still dark, to prepare for the advance. A thick, cold and damp mist clung to the ground adding to the sense of confusion as the various brigades comprising each column shook themselves into some semblance of order. Beyond the line of the Goldbach the French troops too had endured a cold night, stoking their fires with anything combustible they could tear from the nearby villages. Napoleon called his corps commanders to him for their final instructions, the army was ready but initially it was required to play a waiting game; waiting for the Allies to commit themselves. The commanders returned to their men, except Soult, who remained with Napoleon. The timing of Soult's assault on the Pratzen was crucial to the French plan. Davout received revised orders; he was now to march in support of Legrand. Even while this meeting was in progress the battle opened.

ORDERS OF BATTLE

LA GRANDE ARMÉE, AUSTERLITZ, 2 DECEMBER 1805

Commander-in-chief: **L'Empereur Napoléon**
Chief of Staff: **Maréchal Berthier**
Total strength of Army including staff – 74,500
Approx. 605 staff personnel, 58,135 infantry, 11,540 cavalry, 4,220 artillery and train, 157 guns.

IMPERIAL GUARD: MARÉCHAL BESSIÈRES

Total strength approx. 3,885 infantry, 1,130 cavalry, 660 artillery and train, 24 guns.

Infantry of the Imperial Guard
Grenadiers à pied (2 bns.)
Chasseurs à pied (2 bns.)
Royal Italian Guard
Grenadiers à pied (1 bn.)
Chasseurs à pied (1 bn.)

Cavalry of the Imperial Guard
Grenadiers à cheval (4 sqns.)
Chasseurs à cheval (4 sqns.)
Mameluks (½ sqn.)

GRENADIERS DE LA RÉSERVE: GÉNÉRAL DE DIVISION (GD) OUDINOT AND GD DUROC

Total strength approx. 4,650 infantry, 0 cavalry, 340 artillery and train, 8 guns.
Brigade:
1ère Grenadier Régiment (2 bns.) – (3 Gren. coys. and 3 Fus. coys from both 13ème & 58ème Ligne)
2ème Grenadier Régiment (2 bns.) – (3 Gren. coys. and 3 Fus. coys. from both 9ème & 81ème Ligne)
Brigade:
3ème Grenadier Régiment (2 bns.) – (3 Carab. coys. and 3 Chass. coys. from both 2ème & 3ème Légère)
4ème Grenadier Régiment (2 bns.) – (3 Carab. coys. and 3 Chass. coys. from both 28ème & 31ème Légère)
Brigade:
5ème Grenadier Régiment (2 bns.) – (3 Carab. coys. and 3 Chass. coys. from both 12ème & 15ème Légère)

I CORPS: MARÉCHAL BERNADOTTE

Total strength approx. 10,900 infantry, 0 cavalry, 420 artillery and train, 22 guns.

1ère Division: Général de Division (GD) Rivaud de la Raffinière
Brigade: Général de Brigade (GB) Dumoulin
8ème Ligne (3 bns.)
Brigade: GB Pacthod
45ème Ligne (3 bns.)
54ème Ligne (3 bns.)

2ème Division: GD Drouet
Brigade: GB Frere
27ème Légère (3 bns.)
Brigade: GB Werlé
94ème Ligne (3 bns.)
95ème Ligne (3 bns.)

III CORPS: MARÉCHAL DAVOUT

Total strength approx. 3,200 infantry, 830 cavalry, 190 artillery and train, 12 guns.

2ème Division: GD Friant
Brigade: GB Kister
15ème Légère (2 bns. less the voltigeurs)
33ème Ligne (2 bns.)
Brigade: GB Lochet
48ème Ligne (2 bns.)
111ème Ligne (2 bns.)
Brigade: GB Heudelet
15ème Légère (voltigeurs)
108ème Ligne (2 bns.)

4ème Dragon Division: GD Bourcier – Attached to III Corps from the Cavalry Reserve
Brigade: GB Sahuc
15ème Dragons (3 sqns.)
17ème Dragons (3 sqns.)
Brigade: GB Laplanche
18ème Dragons (3 sqns.)
19ème Dragons (3 sqns.)
Brigade: GB Verdière
25ème Dragons (3 sqns.)
27ème Dragons (3 sqns.)

Attached (separately) to III Corps from the 4ème Dragon Division of the Cavalry Reserve
1er Dragons (3 sqns.)

IV CORPS: MARÉCHAL SOULT

Total strength approx. 22,700 infantry, 2,650 cavalry, 1,320 artillery and train, 38 guns.

1ère Division: GD Saint Hilaire
Brigade: GB Morand
10ème Légère (2 bns.)
Brigade: GB Thiébault
14ème Ligne (2 bns.)
35ème Ligne (2 bns.)
Brigade: GB Varé
43ème Ligne (2 bns.)
55ème Ligne (2 bns.)

2ème Division: GD Vandamme
Brigade: GB Schiner
24ème Légère (2 bns.)
Brigade: GB Ferrey
4ème Ligne (2 bns.)
28ème Ligne (2 bns.)
Brigade: GB Candras
46ème Ligne (2 bns.)
57ème Ligne (2 bns.)

3ème Division: GD Legrand
Brigade: GB Merle
26ème Légère (2 bns.)
Tirailleurs du Pô (1 bn.)
Tirailleurs Corses (1 bn.)
Brigade: GB Féry
3 ème Ligne (3 bns.)
Brigade: GB Lavasseur
18ème Ligne (2 bns.)
75ème Ligne (2 bns.)

Light Cavalry Brigade
Brigade: GB Margaron
8ème Hussards (3 sqns.)
11ème Chasseurs à cheval (4 sqns.)
26ème Chasseurs à cheval (3 sqns.)

3ème Dragon Division: GD Beaumont – Attached to IV Corps from the Cavalry Reserve.
Brigade: GB Boyé
5ème Dragons (3 sqns.)
8ème Dragons (3 sqns.)
12ème Dragons (3 sqns.)
Brigade: GB Scalfort
9ème Dragons (3 sqns.)
16ème Dragons (3 sqns.)
21ème Dragons (3 sqns.)

V CORPS: MARÉCHAL LANNES
Total strength approx. 12,800 infantry, 1,130 cavalry, 500 artillery and train, 23 guns.

3ème Division: GD Suchet
Brigade: GB Claparède
17ème Légère (2 bns.)
Brigade: GB Beker
34ème Ligne (2 bns.)
40ème Ligne (2 bns.)
Brigade: GB Valhubert
64ème Ligne (2 bns.)
88ème Ligne (2 bns.)

1ère Division: GD Caffarelli – Attached from III Corps
Brigade: GB Eppler
13ème Légère (2 bns.)
Brigade: GB Demont
17ème Ligne (2 bns.)
30ème Ligne (2 bns.)
Brigade: GB Debilly
51ème Ligne (2 bns.)
61ème Ligne (2 bns.)

2ème Dragon Division: GD Walther – Attached to V Corps from the Cavalry Reserve.
Brigade: GB Sébastiani
3ème Dragons (3 sqns.)
6ème Dragons (3 sqns.)
Brigade: GB Roget
10ème Dragons (3 sqns.)
11ème Dragons (3 sqns.)
Brigade: GB Boussart
13ème Dragons (3 sqns.)
22ème Dragons (3 sqns.)

CAVALRY RESERVE CORPS: MARÉCHAL MURAT
Total strength approx. 5,800 cavalry, 380 artillery and train, 12 guns.

1st Heavy Cavalry Division: GD Nansouty
Brigade: GB Piston
1ère Carabiniers (3 sqns.)
2ème Carabiniers (3 sqns.)
Brigade: GB La Houssaye
2ème Cuirassiers (3 sqns.)
9ème Cuirassiers (3 sqns.)
Brigade: GB Saint-Germain
3ème Cuirassiers (3 sqns.)
12ème Cuirassiers (3 sqns.)

2nd Heavy Cavalry Division: GD d'Hautpoul
Brigade: GB Noirot
1ère Cuirassiers (3 sqns.)
5ème Cuirassiers (3 sqns.)
Brigade: GB Saint-Sulpice
10ème Cuirassiers (3 sqns.)
11ème Cuirassiers (3 sqns.)

Light Cavalry Brigade
Brigade: GB Milhaud
16ème Chasseurs à cheval (3 sqns.)
22ème Chasseurs à cheval (3 sqns.)

Light Cavalry Division: GD Kellermann – Attached to the Cavalry Reserve Corps from I Corps
Brigade: GB Van Marisy
2ème Hussards (3 sqns.)
5ème Hussards (3 sqns.)
Brigade: GB Picard
4ème Hussards (3 sqns.)
5ème Chasseurs à cheval (3 sqns.)

Light Cavalry Division – Attached to the Cavalry Reserve Corps from V Corps
Brigade: GB Treillard
9ème Hussards (3 sqns.)
10ème Hussards (3 sqns.)
Brigade: GB Fauconnet
13ème Chasseurs à cheval (3 sqns.)
21ème Chasseurs à cheval (3 sqns.)

ARTILLERY RESERVE PARK
Total strength approx. 410 artillery and train, 18 guns.

THE AUSTRO-RUSSIAN ARMY, AUSTERLITZ, 2 DECEMBER 1805

Supreme commander at Austerlitz: **Tsar Alexander I**
Commander-in-chief of Allied forces: **Mikhail Kutuzov**
Chief of Staff: **Generalmajor (GM) Weyrother**
Austrian Commander: **Feldmarschalleutant (FML) Prince Liechtenstein**
Observing: **Kaiser Franz I**
Overall Commander of I, II & III Columns: **Lt.Gen. Buxhöwden**
Total strength of Austro-Russian Army excluding general staff – 72,890
Approx. 50,025 infantry, 14,265 cavalry, 7,800 artillery and train, 800 pioneers, 318 guns. *Austrian Army* approx. 16,645 men: 11370 infantry, 3,130 cavalry, 1,715 artillery and train, 430 pioneers, 70 guns. *Russian Army* approx. 56,245 men: 38,655 infantry, 11,135 cavalry, 6,085 artillery and train, 370 pioneers, 248 guns.

(**N.B.** In Austro-Russian formations Austrian units are indicated by **A**)

ARMY ADVANCE GUARD: LT.GEN. BAGRATION
Russian formation
Total strength approx. 7,740 infantry, 4,010 cavalry, 735 artillery and train, 30 guns. (Reinforced by two Austrian batteries at latter stage of battle – 12 guns/approx. 295 personnel)

Brigade:
5. Jäger (3 bns.)
6. Jäger (3 bns.)
Brigade: Maj.Gen. Kamensky II
Archangel Musketeers (3 bns.)
Brigade: Maj.Gen. Engelhardt
Old Ingermanland Musketeers (3 bns.)
Pskov Musketeers (3 bns.)
Brigade: Maj.Gen. Wittgenstein
Pavlograd Hussars (10 sqns.)
Mariupol Hussars (10 sqns.)
Brigade: Maj.Gen. Voropaitzki
Tsarina Leib-Cuirassier (5 sqns.)
Tver Dragoons (5 sqns.)
St. Petersburg Dragoons (3 sqns.)

Attached to Army Advance Guard
Brigade: Maj.Gen. Chaplitz
Khaznenkov Cossacks (5 sqns.)
Kiselev Cossacks (5 sqns.)
Malakhov Cossacks (5 sqns.)

IMPERIAL GUARD: GRAND DUKE CONSTANTINE
Russian formation
Total strength approx. 5400 infantry, 2600 cavalry, 980 artillery and train, 100 pioneers, 40 guns.

Guard Infantry: Lt.Gen. Maliutin
Brigade: Maj.Gen. Depreradovich I
Preobrazhensky Guard (2 bns.)
Semenovsky Guard (2 bns.)
Izmailovsky Guard (2 bns.)
Guard Jäger (1 bn.)
Brigade: Maj.Gen. Lobanov
Guard Grenadiers (3 bns.)
Guard Pioneers (1 coy.)

Guard Cavalry: Lt.Gen. Kologrivov
Brigade: Maj.Gen. Jankovich
Guard Hussars (5 sqns.)
Guard Cossacks (2 sqns.)
Brigade: Maj.Gen. Depreradovich II
Chevalier Garde (5 sqns.)
Horse Guards (5 sqns.)

ADVANCE GUARD OF I COLUMN: FML KIENMAYER
Austro-Russian formation
Total strength approx. 2,450 infantry, 2,340 cavalry, 295 artillery and train, 250 pioneers, 12 guns.

Brigade: GM Carneville
7. Brod-Grenzregiment (1 bn.) – **A**
14. 1 Szeckel-Grenzregiment (2 bns.) – **A**
15. 2 Szeckel-Grenzregiment (2 bns.) – **A**
Brigade: GM Stutterheim
3. O'Reilly-Chevaulegers (8 sqns.) – **A**
1. Merveldt-Uhlanen (¼ sqn.) – **A**
Brigade: GM Nostitz
4. Hessen-Homburg-Husaren (6 sqns.) – **A**
2. Schwarzenberg-Uhlanen (½ sqn.) – **A**
Brigade: GM Moritz Liechtenstein
11. Szeckel-Husaren (6 sqns.) – **A**

Attached to Advance Guard
Sysoev Cossacks (5 sqns.)
Melentev Cossacks (5 sqns.)

I COLUMN: LT.GEN. GENERAL DOKHTUROV
Russian formation
Total strength approx. 7,450 infantry, 210 cavalry, 1,570 artillery and train, 90 pioneers, 64 guns

Brigade: Maj.Gen. Lewis
7. Jäger (1 bn.)
Old Ingermanland Musketeers (3 bns.)
Brigade: Maj.Gen. Urasov
Jaroslav Musketeers (2 bns.)
Vladimir Musketeers (3 bns.)
Briansk Musketeers (3 bns.)
Brigade: Maj.Gen. Lieders
Kiev Grenadiers (3 bns.)
Moscow Musketeers (3 bns.)
Viatsk Musketeers (3 bns.)

Attached to I Column
Denisov Cossacks (5 sqns.)

II COLUMN: LT.GEN. LANGERON
Russian formation
Total strength approx. 9,830 infantry, 360 cavalry, 735 artillery and train, 90 pioneers, 30 guns

Brigade: Maj.Gen. Olsuvev
8. Jäger (2 bns.)
Kursk Musketeers (3 bns.)
Perm Musketeers (3 bns.)
Viborg Musketeers (3 bns.)
Brigade: Maj.Gen. Kamensky
Phanagoria Grenadiers (3 bns.)
Riazan Musketeers (3 bns.)

Attached to II Column
St. Petersburg Dragoons (2 sqns.)
Isayev Cossacks (1 sqn.)

III COLUMN: LT.GEN. PREBYSHEVSKY
Russian formation
Total strength approx. 5,360 infantry, 735 artillery and train, 90 pioneers, 30 guns

Brigade: Maj.Gen. Müller
7. Jäger (2 bns.)
Galicia Musketeers (3 bns.)
Brigade: Maj.Gen Stryk
Boutyrsk Musketeers (3 bns.)
Narva Musketeers (3 bns.)
Brigade: Maj.Gen. Loshakov
8. Jäger (1 bn.)
Azov Musketeers (3 bns.)
Podolsk Musketeers (3 bns.)

IV COLUMN: LT.GEN. MILORADOVICH & FELDZEUGMEISTER (FZM) KOLOWRAT
Austro-Russian formation
Total strength approx. 11,795 infantry (2,875 Russian & 8,920 Austrian), 125 cavalry (Austrian), 1,865 artillery and train, 180 pioneers (Austrian), 76 guns (40 Austrian & 36 Russian)

Advance Guard: Lt.Col. Monakhtin
1. Erzherzog Johann-Dragoner (2 sqns.) – **A**
Apcheron Musketeers (1 bn.)
Novgorod Musketeers (2 bns.)
Brigade: Maj.Gen. Berg
Little Russia Grenadiers (3 bns.)
Novgorod Musketeers (1 bn.)
Brigade: Maj.Gen. Repninsky
Apcheron Musketeers (2 bns.)
Smolensk Musketeers (3 bns.)
Brigade: GM Rottermund
IR20 Kaunitz (1 depot bn.) – **A**
IR23 Salzburg (6 bns.) – **A**
IR24 Auersperg (1 depot bn.) – **A**
Brigade: GM Jurczik
IR1 Kaiser Franz (1 depot bn.) – **A**
IR9 Czartoryski (1 depot bn.) – **A**
IR29 Lindenau (1 bn.) – **A**
IR38 Württemberg (1 bn.) – **A**
IR49 Kerpen (1 depot bn.) – **A**
IR55 Reuss-Greitz (1 depot bn.) – **A**
IR58 Beaulieu (1 bn.) – **A**
(Note: The two coys. of Vienna Jäger normally attached to this formation in Orders of Battle for Austerlitz were not involved in the fighting.)

V COLUMN: FML JOHANN LIECHTENSTEIN
Austro-Russian formation
Total strength approx. 4,620 cavalry (1,165 Austrian & 3,455 Russian), 590 artillery and train, 24 guns (6 Austrian & 18 Russian)

Austrian Cavalry: FML Hohenlohe
Brigade: GM Weber
1. Kaiser-Kürassiere (8 sqns; 2 sqns. detached to Army HQ) – **A**
Brigade: GM Caramelli
5. Nassau-Kürassiere (6 sqns.) – **A**
7. Lothringen-Kürassiere (6 sqns.) – **A**

Russian Cavalry: Lt.Gen. Essen II
Brigade: Maj.Gen. Penitzki
Grand Duke Constantine Uhlans (10 sqns.)
Brigade: Gen.Adj. Uvarov
Elisabethgrad Hussars (10 sqns.)
Kharkov Dragoons (5 sqns.)
Tchernigov Dragoons (5 sqns.)

Attached to V Column
Denisov Cossacks (2½ sqns.)
Gordeev Cossacks (5 sqns.)
Isayev Cossacks (4 sqns.)

THE BATTLE
OF AUSTERLITZ

Feldmarschalleutnant Kienmayer opened the battle when he attacked towards the village of Telnitz with the Advance Guard of I Column. The French put up a tenacious defence, preventing him from taking and holding the village. (Heeresgeschichtliches Museum)

Dokhturov's I Column advanced in support of Kienmayer and with the Russian 7. Jäger committed to the attack the village of Telnitz finally fell into Allied hands. (Philip Haythornthwaite)

THE BATTLE IN THE SOUTH

On the open plain below the Pratzen, on the extreme left of the Allied army, FML Kienmayer had the 5,000 men of his Advance Guard of I Column ready to move sometime before 7.00am. Sending some squadrons of 4. Hessen-Homburg Husaren ahead to scout the approaches to Telnitz, Kienmayer learnt that the French were defending a low hill in front of the village. Behind the hill, reaching down to the village, were a tangle of vineyards surrounded by a ditch. The 3ème Ligne from Legrand's division of IV Corps prepared to defend this strong position, supported by a cavalry brigade under General Margaron. Kienmayer probed forward with 2nd Battalion 1. Szeckel Grenzers and as they emerged from the mist the French line erupted into action inflicting horrendous casualties on the Austrians. The first battalion of the Grenzer regiment came forward in support with two cavalry regiments. The two battalions, working together, drove the French back into Telnitz, but it was clear that it would not be as easy to brush aside the French as Weyrother had imagined. Kienmayer fed in his last three battalions, but there was no sign of Dokhturov and the main body of I Column who should by now have been in a position to assist. The Grenz infantry finally gained the village, only to be pushed out again. Then, about an hour after the action had begun, Buxhöwden, the overall commander of the left wing, approached with Dokhturov's I Column. Buxhöwden ordered a brigade forward; the 7. Jäger to support the attack and the three battalions of the New Ingermanland regiment to form a reserve. Reinforced, the Allies attacked the village once more with two Grenz battalions and the Russian Jäger. Suffering mounting casualties and now facing overwhelming numbers the order was given for 3ème Ligne to evacuate Telnitz. The French reformed in battle order west of the Goldbach supported by Mangeron's cavalry and artillery, now positioned on high-ground north-west of Telnitz. Although Kienmayer's orders were to press on over the stream, Buxhöwden told him to wait. The plan called for the columns to advance in unison and the position of II Column was unclear. A brief period of calm descended on Telnitz.

Up on the plateau confusion reigned. The late hour of the final meeting and the necessity to draft maps with orders in German and Russian ensured desperate staff officers were still distributing orders after 7.00am, the time specified for the beginning of the advance. The thick fog and sprawling encampments made the task difficult enough, but the fact that some Russian officers had left their commands during the night for more comfortable billets in the villages behind the plateau, further compounded the issue.

The Battles for Sokolnitz and Telnitz

Eventually Langeron's II Column was led forward through the fog down the gentle slope in the general direction of their initial target, the Goldbach stream between Telnitz and Sokolnitz, to the right of I Column. Ahead of them initially stood two weak battalions – the Tirailleurs du Pô and Tirailleurs Corses – but the sound of gunfire from Telnitz alerted General Legrand, the divisional commander on the southern flank, to the developing situation. He ordered the two battalions of 26ème Légère to Sokolnitz and General Lavasseur's brigade (two battalions from both 18ème and 75ème Ligne) to cover the area from Kobelnitz towards the

One of the dominating granaries in Sokolnitz, close to the castle, possession of which was contested fiercely throughout the day of the battle.

Pheasantry, a large walled park about three-quarters of a mile to the south. All his troops were now committed to the defence of the Goldbach line. His men had just taken up their position when the leading brigade of Langeron's Column, having veered to the right of their intended line, loomed up in front of Sokolnitz. Aware that the French were occupying the village, Langeron ordered the brigade to deploy and open fire on the defenders, supported by their battalion guns, while he awaited the rest of his command. While this bombardment took place Prebyshevsky's III Column came into view having been delayed further by the soft clinging mud of the ploughed fields on the slopes below Pratze village. Finding Langeron much closer than he expected Prebyshevsky formed his column to the right of II Column, facing Sokolnitz Castle, a large country house surrounded by a wall with massive stone outbuildings, north of the village. Three companies of second battalion 26ème Légère defended the castle while the rest of the battalion was drawn up to the rear on high ground with artillery support.

Determined to waste no more time Prebyshevsky ordered a brigade under Major-General Müller to take the castle. A battalion of 7. Jäger and three battalions of the Galicia Musketeers advanced on the castle and easily drove away the defenders who fell back to the main body of their battalion. The disorganised Russians now came under close-range

The second battalion of 26ème Légère charge into Sokolnitz and recapture the castle from Major-General Müller's Brigade of III Column. A swift Russian counterattack, typical of the fighting in Sokolnitz, then ejected the 26ème Légère in turn. (Girbal – Sammlung Alfred und Roland Umhey)

OVERLEAF

THE BATTLE FOR TELNITZ. The small village of Telnitz on the banks of the Goldbach stream was destined to play a vital role in the Battle of Austerlitz. An Allied attempt to secure the village during the freezing night before the battle failed, leaving the French in possession. Anything that would burn was stripped from the houses to help warm the soldiers through the night. The attack on Telnitz began at about 7.00am. With a thick mist still covering the ground FML Kienmayer ordered his Advance Guard to capture the village. The defenders, men of the French 3ème Ligne, resisted ferociously from a low hill outside the village but repeated assaults by Austrian troops forced the French defenders back amongst the shattered houses. Further attacks ejected them completely but they quickly rallied, counter-attacked and regained the village. With the brilliant sunrise beginning to filter through the thinning mist Russian Jäger from the main body of I Column joined the attack while the rest of the force waited in reserve. Despite their heroic resistance, the men of 3ème Ligne could not maintain their position and evacuated Telnitz. (Christa Hook)

artillery fire, which wounded Müller, and a countercharge by the second battalion 26ème Légère regained the castle for the French. The Russians in turn counter-attacked with the weakened battalions of Major-General Stryk's Brigade and threw back 26ème Légère once more.

To their left Langeron had curtailed his bombardment of Sokolnitz village and ordered an infantry assault. His second brigade had still not appeared so the task fell to Major-General Olsuvev. Nine of his 11 battalions were committed, with just two battalions of the Kursk Musketeer Regiment in reserve. Leading with 8. Jäger and Viborg Musketeers, Olsuvev engaged the first battalion of 26ème Légère, and after a brief but ferocious struggle the French were driven out of the southern end of the town and retreated into unexpected danger. The remaining four Russian battalions swept into Sokolnitz and, with the town cleared, turned to the north. Here they added their weight to that of Stryk's Brigade of III Column, arrayed against the re-forming 2nd Battalion of 26ème Légère, Tirailleurs du Pô and Tirailleurs Corses. Faced by ten battalions, in all about 4,000 men, the French fell back.

While the fight for Sokolnitz had been taking place, the battle for Telnitz flared up once more. From the early hours of the morning Davout had been driving the leading elements of III Corps on as fast as the exhausted men and horses could go. The pace of the march from Vienna had been tough and many had fallen by the wayside. Davout was heading for Sokolnitz but, receiving a request for help from the French

right at Telnitz, he despatched General Heudelet's Infantry Brigade of Friant's Division and General Bourcier's Dragoon Division to their assistance. The rest of his force pressed on towards Sokolnitz. It was about 9.00am when Heudelet's Brigade (two voltigeur companies 15ème Légère and two battalions 108ème Ligne) halted to re-form close to Telnitz. The fog still blanketed the ground when the brigade emerged from it and burst into the village. The Russian 7. Jäger fell back in confusion onto a Grenzer battalion and these two battalions in turn fled, disordering the New Ingermanland Musketeer Regiment standing in reserve. This outbreak of firing in the fog and the sudden appearance of fleeing men amongst them caused these Russian soldiers to join the rout. The breathless but elated soldiers of 108ème Ligne briefly took possession of the body-strewn hill east of Telnitz before becoming a target themselves. Deployed to the right of the Allies' reserve were six squadrons of 4. Hessen–Homburg Husaren. They had already suffered a number of casualties that morning from French skirmishers around Telnitz, so when two squadrons received the order to charge they did so with relish. The 108ème suffered heavily; unable to offer any resistance the survivors fled back through the vineyards and village, turning north towards Sokolnitz, the *voltigeurs* preventing any pursuit. However, the horror did not end there; as they moved northwards they ran into a new storm of fire. This time the 'enemy' was the first battalion 26ème Légère. Driven from Sokolnitz by Olsuvev's men and surprised by this body of men rushing towards them through the fog and smoke of battle, the 26ème Légère opened fire on their comrades. Eventually order was restored but the 108ème had seen enough for one day and took no further part in the battle.

Desperate Fighting in Sokolnitz

The Allies took possession of Telnitz once more and advanced their cavalry across the Goldbach. Kienmayer was keen to push on, but Buxhöwden would not sanction it until he heard that II and III Columns had moved past Sokolnitz. As the gunfire around Telnitz died down, the battle for Sokolnitz flared up again, rejoined with a far greater desperation than before. Some of the battalions of II and III Columns that had eventually cleared the French out of Sokolnitz had become intermingled and with the fog still hanging in the low ground it was taking time to reorganise the commands. The French now threw in a new devastating attack. After despatching Heudelet's Brigade towards Telnitz, Davout and Friant had pushed on and were now close to Sokolnitz. Informed that the Allies were occupying the village and castle, Davout ordered Friant to recapture them. It was probably a little before 10.00am. General Lochet's Brigade led the attack, from the west. With 48ème Ligne in front and the 111ème Ligne moving forward on their left in support, the French smashed into the re-forming Russian battalions. The leading regiment driving back the Perm Musketeers and the grenadier battalion of Kursk Musketeers while the second hit 8. Jäger and Viborg Musketeers. As these men tumbled from the village Langeron rode amongst them, rallied them and sent them back into battle. The 111ème were promptly driven back out of the village but the 48ème, though also driven back, tenaciously held on to the southern end of the village. Friant then sent in his last brigade, commanded by

General Kister. The 15ème Légère attacked the north-western end of the village, pushing through the first resistance before encountering the grenadier battalion of the Kursk Musketeers. This time the Russians stood their ground and the battle broke down into a series of vicious individual hand-to-hand combats amongst the shattered buildings. The last battalion of Kister's Brigade, 33ème Ligne, bore down on the castle. The Russians of Major-General Stryk's Brigade fell back before the fresh onslaught, regrouped and returned to the fray. However, all along the Sokolnitz line the aggressive tactics and determination displayed by the outnumbered French prevented the Russians from gaining the advantage. The battle flowed backwards and forwards, each side momentarily gaining the upper hand before the pendulum swung back the other way. Between Telnitz and Sokolnitz some 13,000 Allied infantry had been directly involved in the attack on the line of the Goldbach; they were held back by about 7,000 determined Frenchmen. However, rather worryingly for the Allies there was as yet no sign of IV Column, which should by now have been bearing down on Kobelnitz to the right of III Column. For while this struggle was taking place on the Goldbach, IV Column was involved in events elsewhere that were to determine the final outcome of the battle and the fate of the Austro-Russian army.

THE BATTLE IN THE CENTRE

Marshal Soult attacks the Pratzen Plateau

Confusion appears to have been the order of the day on the northern end of the Pratzen plateau in the early hours of 2 December. It seems that the overnight encampments of Liechtenstein's cavalry column (V Column) spread over a wider area than intended. Although some were at the foot of the Pratzen on the lower eastern slopes, others appear to have been up on the plateau itself. When the order to move came, V Column marched for the open country north of the Pratzen, towards Blasowitz. In the process they traversed the formation area of III Corps, and possibly IV Corps, disrupting their preparations. It was for this reason that III Column commenced their advance later than I and II Columns. The march of IV Column was due to take place an hour later than the other columns as the distance it was required to cover was less. Although the strongest column in numbers (about 12,000 men), IV Column suffered in quality. The column was composed of both Russian and Austrian troops under the joint control of Russian Lieutenant-General Miloradovich and Austrian *Feldzeugmeister* Kolowrat. All 14 Russian battalions had marched to Braunau and back, reducing their average strength to a much depleted 240 men, while a large number of the Austrian battalions were the regiment's depot battalions formed of semi-invalids and new recruits with only the most limited degree of training. Alexander rode up while IV Column made its final dispositions and urged Kutuzov to set it in motion. Although III Column was not yet in place he felt unable to oppose the Tsar and ordered Miloradovich to send the advance guard forward. It was about 9.00am when the staff officer leading the way across the plateau towards Pratze observed movement below in the low ground in front of the villages of Puntowitz and Jirzikowitz.

TOP **Feldzeugmeister Kolowrat-Krakowsky, the 57-year-old joint commander of IV Column at Austerlitz. Kolowrat, a veteran of the Turkish wars, led the main Austrian infantry force of almost 9,000 men. (Heeresgeschichtliches Museum)**

ABOVE **Lieutenant-General M.A. Miloradovich, the 34-year-old Russian joint commander of IV Column. Miloradovich had served in Italy (1799) under the great Russian general Suvorov and had fought at Dürnstein in November as the Russians had fallen back from Braunau.**

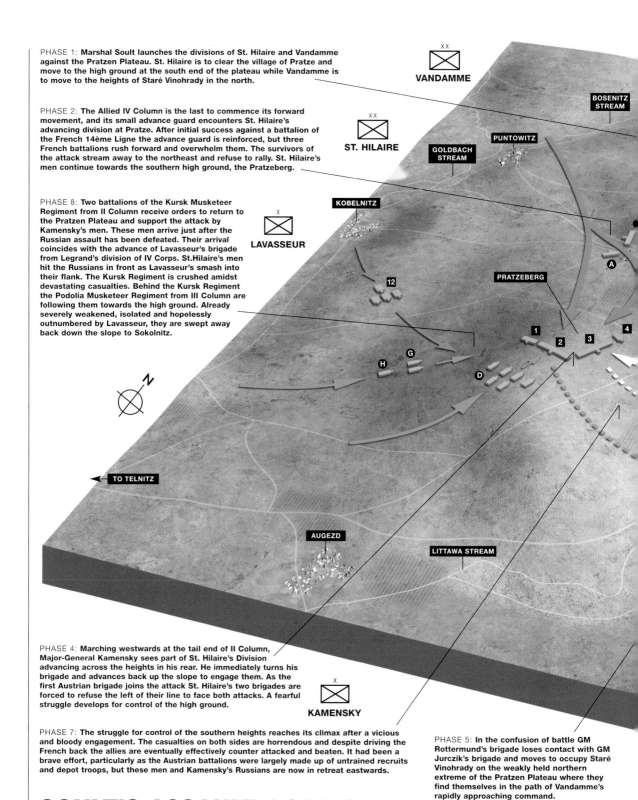

PHASE 1: **Marshal Soult launches the divisions of St. Hilaire and Vandamme against the Pratzen Plateau. St. Hilaire is to clear the village of Pratze and move to the high ground at the south end of the plateau while Vandamme is to move to the heights of Staré Vinohrady in the north.**

PHASE 2: **The Allied IV Column is the last to commence its forward movement, and its small advance guard encounters St. Hilaire's advancing division at Pratze. After initial success against a battalion of the French 14ème Ligne the advance guard is reinforced, but three French battalions rush forward and overwhelm them. The survivors of the attack stream away to the northeast and refuse to rally. St. Hilaire's men continue towards the southern high ground, the Pratzeberg.**

PHASE 8: **Two battalions of the Kursk Musketeer Regiment from II Column receive orders to return to the Pratzen Plateau and support the attack by Kamensky's men. These men arrive just after the Russian assault has been defeated. Their arrival coincides with the advance of Lavasseur's brigade from Legrand's division of IV Corps. St.Hilaire's men hit the Russians in front as Lavasseur's smash into their flank. The Kursk Regiment is crushed amidst devastating casualties. Behind the Kursk Regiment the Podolia Musketeer Regiment from III Column are following them towards the high ground. Already severely weakened, isolated and hopelessly outnumbered by Lavasseur, they are swept away back down the slope to Sokolnitz.**

VANDAMME

ST. HILAIRE

LAVASSEUR

KAMENSKY

BOSENITZ STREAM

PUNTOWITZ

GOLDBACH STREAM

KOBELNITZ

PRATZEBERG

TO TELNITZ

AUGEZD

LITTAWA STREAM

PHASE 4: **Marching westwards at the tail end of II Column, Major-General Kamensky sees part of St. Hilaire's Division advancing across the heights in his rear. He immediately turns his brigade and advances back up the slope to engage them. As the first Austrian brigade joins the attack St. Hilaire's two brigades are forced to refuse the left of their line to face both attacks. A fearful struggle develops for control of the high ground.**

PHASE 7: **The struggle for control of the southern heights reaches its climax after a vicious and bloody engagement. The casualties on both sides are horrendous and despite driving the French back the allies are eventually effectively counter attacked and beaten. It had been a brave effort, particularly as the Austrian battalions were largely made up of untrained recruits and depot troops, but these men and Kamensky's Russians are now in retreat eastwards.**

PHASE 5: **In the confusion of battle GM Rottermund's brigade loses contact with GM Jurczik's brigade and moves to occupy Staré Vinohrady on the weakly held northern extreme of the Pratzen Plateau where they find themselves in the path of Vandamme's rapidly approaching command.**

SOULT'S ASSAULT AGAINST THE AUSTRO-RUSSIAN CENTRE

2 December 1805, 9.00am–11.00am, viewed from the south-east, showing Marshal Soult's assault on the centre of the Allied line and the desperate struggle for the Pratzen Plateau.

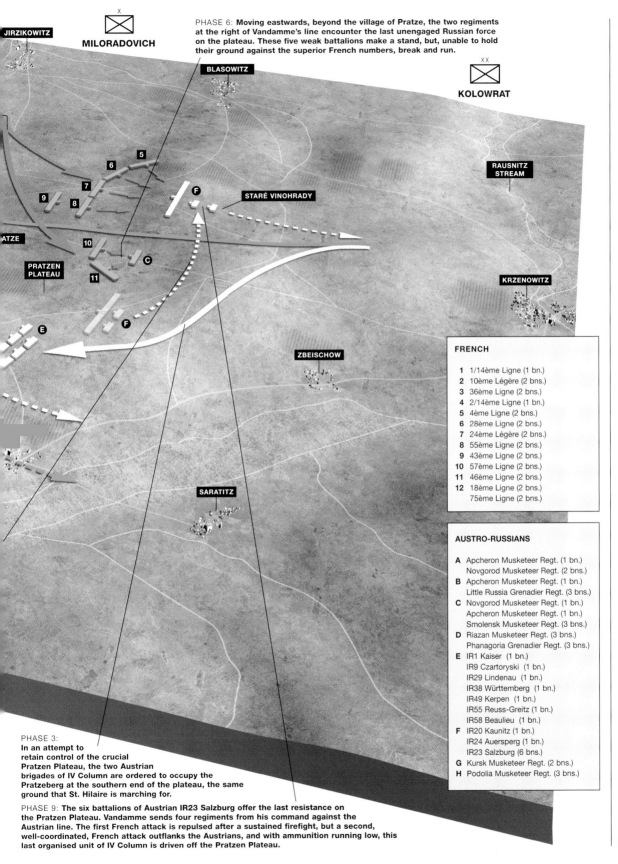

JIRZIKOWITZ

X
MILORADOVICH

BLASOWITZ

PHASE 6: Moving eastwards, beyond the village of Pratze, the two regiments at the right of Vandamme's line encounter the last unengaged Russian force on the plateau. These five weak battalions make a stand, but, unable to hold their ground against the superior French numbers, break and run.

X X
KOLOWRAT

5
6
7
9
8

F

STARÉ VINOHRADY

RAUSNITZ
STREAM

ATZE

10

C

PRATZEN
PLATEAU

11

KRZENOWITZ

E

F

ZBEISCHOW

SARATITZ

FRENCH

1	1/14ème Ligne (1 bn.)
2	10ème Légère (2 bns.)
3	36ème Ligne (2 bns.)
4	2/14ème Ligne (1 bn.)
5	4ème Ligne (2 bns.)
6	28ème Ligne (2 bns.)
7	24ème Légère (2 bns.)
8	55ème Ligne (2 bns.)
9	43ème Ligne (2 bns.)
10	57ème Ligne (2 bns.)
11	46ème Ligne (2 bns.)
12	18ème Ligne (2 bns.)
	75ème Ligne (2 bns.)

AUSTRO-RUSSIANS

A	Apcheron Musketeer Regt. (1 bn.)
	Novgorod Musketeer Regt. (2 bns.)
B	Apcheron Musketeer Regt. (1 bn.)
	Little Russia Grenadier Regt. (3 bns.)
C	Novgorod Musketeer Regt. (1 bn.)
	Apcheron Musketeer Regt. (1 bn.)
	Smolensk Musketeer Regt. (3 bns.)
D	Riazan Musketeer Regt. (3 bns.)
	Phanagoria Grenadier Regt. (3 bns.)
E	IR1 Kaiser (1 bn.)
	IR9 Czartoryski (1 bn.)
	IR29 Lindenau (1 bn.)
	IR38 Württemberg (1 bn.)
	IR49 Kerpen (1 bn.)
	IR55 Reuss-Greitz (1 bn.)
	IR58 Beaulieu (1 bn.)
F	IR20 Kaunitz (1 bn.)
	IR24 Auersperg (1 bn.)
	IR23 Salzburg (6 bns.)
G	Kursk Musketeer Regt. (2 bns.)
H	Podolia Musketeer Regt. (3 bns.)

PHASE 3:
In an attempt to retain control of the crucial Pratzen Plateau, the two Austrian brigades of IV Column are ordered to occupy the Pratzeberg at the southern end of the plateau, the same ground that St. Hilaire is marching for.

PHASE 9: The six battalions of Austrian IR23 Salzburg offer the last resistance on the Pratzen Plateau. Vandamme sends four regiments from his command against the Austrian line. The first French attack is repulsed after a sustained firefight, but a second, well-coordinated, French attack outflanks the Austrians, and with ammunition running low, this last organised unit of IV Column is driven off the Pratzen Plateau.

The French infantry of Soult's IV Corps await the order to advance. Positioned in low-lying ground around the villages of Puntowitz and Jirzikowitz, shrouded in the early morning mist, they were invisible to the Allies on the plateau. (Girbal – Sammlung Alfred und Roland Umhey)

Initially he thought it was the tail end of III Column, off course, then he realised the truth.

From his battlefield headquarters on the Zuran hill Napoleon had peered blindly ahead into the grey since dawn. The thick fog that descended during the night had spread like a shroud over the Pratzen plateau. It was just over three miles to the village of Pratze, a little further to the high ground of Staré Vinohrady, but nothing was visible. Then, around 8.00am the sun rose, like a great golden orb according to those who saw it, and slowly the fog on the plateau melted away and the shroud evaporated. It was clear to Napoleon that the Allied left was moving off the plateau to the south as he had hoped. Now it was important to choose the right time to launch the attack on the vacated position. Although the fog was lifting from the high ground, in the hollows around Puntowitz and Jirzikowitz it still mingled with the smoke from countless campfires and provided a cloak of invisibility for the two divisions of Soult's IV Corps standing silently, waiting. On the left stood Vandamme's brigades, to the right those of St. Hilaire. When their time came they were to gain the plateau as swiftly as possible from where they could wheel north or south into the rear of the Austro-Russian army. As Napoleon waited the sound of gunfire filled the air to the south and now artillery fire joined on the northern flank too as the guns of Lannes, V Corps engaged Bagration's command. The entire frontline, some seven miles long, echoed to the sound of battle. It was around 9.00am when he gave the order for Soult's 16,000 men to march.

Back on the plateau the horrifying news that the French were advancing brought a flurry of orders. For the first time in many days the Allies recognised the truth; the French were not preparing to retreat at all; they were intent on battle. Yet it was also a shock for the French. Soult's orders informed him that the Allies had abandoned the Pratzen plateau and moved to the south. The small advance guard of 650 Russian infantry (the remnants of three battalions) took up defensive positions around Pratze, supported by two weak squadrons of the Austrian Erzherzog Johann dragoons. Then, on the suggestion of an Austrian staff colonel, Baron Wimpffen, it was determined to occupy and hold the high ground of the Pratzeberg at the southern end of the plateau. With Alexander's approval Kutuzov ordered FZM Kolowrat to move southwards with his two Austrian brigades to secure this position while Miloradovitch's Russian brigades would defend Pratze and the Staré Vinohrady, the high point at the northern end of the plateau.

It appears that St. Hilaire's brigades pushed on more rapidly than Vandamme's command. General Thiébault was ordered to clear Pratze to which task he allocated the first battalion of 14ème Ligne. Anticipating little opposition the battalion, about 750 men, advanced straight for the village supported by two artillery pieces. Lying in wait about 250 men of the Novgorod Musketeers destroyed the attack, with the supporting grenadier battalion of Apcheron Musketeers and three battalions of Little Russia Grenadiers combining to capture the guns. Before these Russians had time to re-form, the second wave of Thiébault's Brigade swept forward through the outnumbered and disorganised Russians and recaptured the guns. Both Russian brigade commanders, Major-Generals Berg and Repninsky, were wounded before five Russian battalions turned and fled, only the efforts of the two squadrons of Austrian dragoons preventing the French pursuit. However, these Russians had suffered greatly in the campaign already and even the efforts of Alexander and Kutuzov failed to stop their flight to the rear.

Bloody struggle for the Pratzeberg

Meanwhile, the 10ème Légère, the leading element of St. Hilaire's Division followed orders, by passed Pratze and continued on to secure the Pratzeberg. As they had moved west of the village and began ascending the slopes towards their goal, Major-General Kamensky, the Russian officer commanding the brigade of II Column that Langeron was awaiting, turned as he marched on Sokolnitz and observed this threatening movement by 10ème Légère. Sending this information to Langeron he immediately wheeled his brigade and headed back up the slope to intercept the French. Kamensky's force was strong, three battalions each of the Phanagoria Grenadier Regiment and Riazan Musketeer Regiment, about 3,800 men. The 10ème could muster about 1,500.

Faced with this pressure to their front, the 10ème began a fighting withdrawal as the Russians attempted to use their greater numbers to outflank and turn the French right. As the Russians were closing St. Hilaire rushed forward with the rallied 1st Battalion of 14ème Ligne and positioned them on the threatened flank. Then Thiébault led forward the rest of his brigade and formed them on the left of 10ème Légère, preparing to engage Kamensky's Russians. Varé's brigade waited at Pratze for Vandamme. However, just as the whole weight of the French line aligned against Kamensky, a large body of unidentified troops approached from the east. On closer inspection it was clear they were wearing helmets but their greatcoats hid their uniforms. An officer shouted at the French not to fire as they were Bavarians. St. Hilaire consulted with Thiébault, both unsure what action to take. Initially they redeployed the line, pivoting the left back on the 10ème so as to face the potential new threat. The line, already strengthened by six pieces of artillery, was bolstered further by the arrival of six 12-pdrs from IV Corps reserve. As these new arrivals moved into the line an officer from the 'Bavarians' broke away from the main body and spoke to a Russian officer. It was now clear that the new arrivals were not Bavarians but Austrians. It was the brigade of GM Jurczik, part of Kolowrat's command despatched to take control of the Pratzeberg when the French had first shown themselves in front of Pratze. To their right rear GM Rottermund's Brigade formed in support. These two brigades mustered 15 battalions but seven of them were depot battalions. After the initial French attack on Pratze had turned towards the Pratzeberg, Kutuzov

LEFT **A view of the battle for the Pratzen plateau from Napoleon's headquarters. Pratze is in flames in the centre while all around the struggle for control of the high ground is evident.**

BELOW **A view from the Pratzeberg down to the village of Pratze. The French 10ème Légère advanced across this ground while the rest of St. Hilaire's Division was fighting for control of the village against Miloradovich's men.**

The fierce and bloody battle for the Pratzeberg. Kamensky's Russians and Jurczik's Austrians engage St.Hilaire's Division at close range. (Frantisek Richter – Sammlung Alfred und Roland Umhey)

had ridden south, and with Weyrother was on hand to help bolster these raw troops.

There is some confusion evident in accounts of the fighting on the Pratzen plateau, perhaps because it extended across three miles of undulating terrain and broke down into two distinct areas: the fight for the Pratzeberg in the south and the fight for Staré Vinohrady in the north. It appears that the raw Austrian battalions of GM Jurczik's brigade advanced bravely and steadily in line up the slope towards the French position. Kamensky's Russian Brigade marched forward too. The French held their fire before unleashing a storm of canister and musketry, tearing great holes in the advancing lines. The Allies fell back in some disarray, Jurczik's Brigade pulling away to their left closer to the Russians. Rottermund's Brigade, which had been advancing in support, led by the Grenadiers of IR23 Salzburg, now found themselves alone in the smoke and confusion and withdrew back towards the Allied position on Staré Vinohrady. With the threat from the east apparently removed, St. Hilaire formed his men in one line again and followed up Kamensky's retreating brigade. However, the Russians re-formed as did Jurczik's Austrians, and prepared to engage the French once more. A terrific firefight now developed with the French, having advanced, becoming isolated. The numerous Allied staff officers present realised that the French were getting the best of the musketry and so prepared for a combined Russian and Austrian bayonet attack. The advance began, with the Russians on the left shouting loudly as they moved forward with the more sedate Austrians

The land between the Sokolnitz pheasantry and the Pratzeberg. Langeron rushed the Kursk Musketeers and Podolia Musketeers towards the Pratzeberg to join the fight, but they arrived too late and faced the victorious French alone. (Martin Worel)

moving forward on their right. St. Hilaire poured a continual fire of musketry into the Allied ranks, slowing their advance considerably, yet inexorably it edged closer, returning fire all the time. Jurczik received a fatal wound, while Weyrother had a horse shot from under him. Casualties were mounting all around as the Russians desperately pressed ahead trying to come to grips with the French. St. Hilaire's men were suffering badly too and the constant pressure from the Allies forced them to slowly give ground back towards their artillery. While this action had been progressing, Langeron rode up from Sokolnitz to see for himself what was developing. Coming up to Kamensky's brigade while it was engaged with the French he recognised the seriousness of the situation and rode off to find reinforcements, which he found in the form of two battalions of the Kursk Musketeer Regiment, the only uncommitted battalions of his Column. Immediately he ordered them up to the Pratzen plateau.

St. Hilaire's men had withdrawn to a position they considered suitable to make a stand but the Allied attack ground towards them despite the increasing carnage in the closely packed ranks. The Phanagoria Grenadiers and Riazan Musketeers made another series of desperate bayonet attacks on the French line determined to destroy their opposition while the previously untried Austrian battalions kept up a regular if ill-directed fire. The French were suffering heavily now but it is possible that they received support from 43ème Ligne of Varé's brigade. A bullet wounded St. Hilaire, another killed the colonel of 14ème Ligne and Thiébault lost two horses shot from under him. However, it was close to two hours since the French had first approached Pratze and both sides were running low on ammunition. St. Hilaire had been considering retreating again, but after a short conference with his senior officers it was decided that a bayonet attack of their own was the only way they could extricate their battalions from this increasingly threatening situation. Aware that the Allied rate of fire was slowing down St. Hilaire ordered his two brigades to attack. As soon as the order was given the French line stormed forward. Kamensky's men had been attacking constantly for almost two hours without breaking the French line, now, having suffered heavy casualties, they were all but out of ammunition and facing a fresh attack. Both regiments broke and ran. The brave Kamensky became a prisoner but very few others joined him as the bayonet did its work. Langeron, who had been urging the attacks on extricated himself and rode off to find Buxhöwden to acquaint him with the fearful news. He later claimed that his senior commander was under the influence of alcohol when he found him and refused to acknowledge the desperate nature of the situation.

Although the Russians took the main force of the attack, some of the Austrian battalions made a stand in the face of this onslaught. The depot battalion of IR49 Kerpen and a battalion of IR58 Beaulieu formed *masse* together and fired on the oncoming French, forcing a temporary halt. However, IR58 was attacked and thrown back. The battalion of IR49 then launched an attack with the depot battalion of IR55 Reuss-Greitz, coming under a heavy fire as they did so. The attack faltered as IR49 began to waver although the battalion commander prevented his men from breaking. They kept up volley fire, which deterred the French from closing, but in the meantime IR55, having lost their commanding officer and a number of other officers, fell back. Standing alone, IR49 Kerpen had no choice but to join the retreat.

With the Pratzeberg now clear of Allied troops Langeron's two battalions of the Kursk Musketeers finally approached the scene of battle. St. Hilaire's men re-formed to face this new enemy as support arrived from Lavasseur's Brigade of Legrand's Division, which had been in reserve near Kobelnitz. Seeing the movement of the Kursk Musketeers, Lavasseur advanced with all four battalions (18ème and 75ème Ligne). The Russians, numbering about 1,200 men, were first struck on their left flank by about 3,000 men then assaulted in front by St.Hilaire and collapsed. The survivors of the Kursk Musketeers fled for safety. As these men made good their escape another Russian regiment arrived, the Podolia Musketeers from III Corps, now the only formed Allied unit on the southern extreme of the Pratzen. They had already experienced a tough campaign with all three battalions together mustering only about 500 men. Lavasseur turned his brigade to face them and outnumbering the Russians by about six to one there was only one possible outcome. The survivors of the Podolia fled for safety and took cover behind the walls of the Sokolnitz pheasantry. St. Hilaire and his exhausted command were finally masters of the Pratzeberg.

While the fighting here came to a conclusion that at the northern end of the plateau was reaching a climax.

Last resistance on the Pratzen Plateau

After St. Hilaire's initial attack on Pratze there was a short lull around the village as Vandamme brought his division up to where Varé held his brigade. Vandamme bypassed Pratze on the northern side. Just over a mile ahead, on the highest point of Staré Vinohrady, a solid line of Austrian infantry stood determinedly in his path. These men, GM Rottermund's Brigade, separated from the rest of Kolowrat's command during the attack on the Pratzeberg, had fallen back and regrouped on the high ground at the northern end of the plateau under cover of Miloradovich's men. However, with St. Hilaire's successful storming of Pratze, the Russians had suffered a dramatic reduction of their strength.

TOP **A view of the ground over which Vandamme's men advanced. The higher ground on the left horizon is Staré Vinohrady and that on the right horizon is the Pratzeberg. Control of these two highpoints was crucial to the outcome of the battle.**

ABOVE **Général de division Vandamme led his division towards Staré Vinohrady at the northern end of the Pratzen plateau, passing to the left of Pratze. In their path stood the remnants of Miloradovich's command.**

The only units still in the field under Miloradovich's control were five battalions (three of the Smolensk Musketeer Regiment, the grenadier battalion of the Novgorod Musketeers and a musketeer battalion of the Apcheron Musketeers), numbering only about 1,000 men, with supporting battalion artillery, the rest having fled. These men were first to feel the weight of Vandamme's attack.

Vandamme moved his division forward with each brigade aligned on the next, Schiner's on the left (two battalions 24ème Légère), Férey's in the centre (two battalions of both 4ème and 28ème Ligne) and Candras' on the right (two battalions of both 46ème and 57ème Ligne). As they bypassed Pratze, Candras' Brigade discovered Miloradovich's Russians in their path. Vandamme halted his division then advanced Candras' Brigade, boasting 3,000 men, against the thin line of Russians to their front. As the brigade approached the Russian line the 57ème halted and a number of artillery pieces opened fire. While this bombardment was taking place, the 46ème moved to the right to outflank the outnumbered Russians. Once in position the two regiments closed to musket range and unleashed a devastating fire. The Russians replied briefly, getting off a few artillery rounds before the pressure from two sides became too intense and the line broke and fled. As on the Pratzeberg the French bayoneted many of the wounded Russians rather than take them prisoner.

Vandamme now ordered the 24ème Légère to deploy into skirmish formation, swarm forward through the vineyards covering Staré Vinohrady and dislodge the Austrians on the high ground. This formation now represented the last Allied force still operational on the Pratzen plateau. All six battalions of IR23 Salzburg, the only Austrian infantry regiment at the battle with more than one battalion present, formed the first line. Although the facts are unclear it is possible that IR24 Auersperg formed a second line in support to their rear. IR 23 numbered about 3,000 men and stood its ground well, firing regular volleys at the elusive Frenchmen probing at the front and flanks of the line. Despite IR23 presenting such a clear target, the 24ème were unable to overcome the regiment's determined stand, commanded by *Oberst* Stendahl. Failing to make progress Vandamme recalled the 24ème. But the respite was only temporary. The French regrouped and Vandamme ordered a more concerted attack on the stubborn Austrians. This time instead of two battalions he attacked with eight, totalling about

ABOVE **The high point of Staré Vinohrady where six battalions of Austrian IR23 Salzburg made their stand. Vandamme's men attacked from the left of the photo against the Austrian line. (Martin Worel)**

LEFT **Napoleon, observing the action on the Pratzen plateau from his position on Zuran, awaits news of Soult's success before ordering forward Bernadotte's I Corps. With the plateau apparently secure Napoleon rode forward to Staré Vinohrady. (Sammlung Alfred und Roland Umhey)**

6,000 men. Forming his battalions in one line Vandamme urged his men forward. On the far left of the line were 4ème Ligne, in the centre 28ème Ligne and 24ème Légère, while on the right 55ème Ligne were called forward from Varé's supporting brigade. Moving forward slowly through the vineyards, taking heavy casualties from artillery fire, this force eventually arrived in a position where its flanking battalions could overlap the Austrian line. Once in musket range IR23 poured murderous volleys into the encircling French line. Vandamme halted the advance and exchanged volleys, but with his muskets outnumbering those of IR23 by two-to-one and Stendahl's men beginning to run low on ammunition, the volume of Austrian fire decreased and casualties mounted. As this pressure increased, the resistance of IR23 finally broke and the line collapsed. The formed battalion of IR24 Auersperg covering their retreat prevented any energetic pursuit by Vandamme's men. It was about 11.00am and after a series of battles lasting two hours the Pratzen plateau from north to south was in the possession of Napoleon's army. Napoleon, still positioned on Zuran hill, received news of Soult's success and prepared to move his headquarters to Staré Vinohrady. Before moving he issued orders for Bernadotte to move I

The commander of the advance guard of the Allied army, Peter Bagration, had been promoted to Lieutenant-General following his successful delay of the French pursuit at Schöngrabern. Now he formed the right flank of the army, waiting until the Allies' flanking move was under way before commencing his own advance.

Feldmarschalleutnant Johann Liechtenstein, the Austrian commander of V Column, a mixed force of Russian and Austrian cavalry. Liechtenstein's cavalry arrived late at their start position due to confusion on the plateau. (David Hollins)

Corps eastwards, Drouet's Division moving up to the Pratzen plateau while Rivaud's Division advanced to their left and almost immediately became involved in the fighting on the northern flank. He also issued orders for his reserve, the Imperial Guard and Reserve Grenadiers to march towards the Pratzen.

From his new position on Staré Vinohrady Napoleon was about to witness the last great attempt to change the course of the battle; the attack of the Russian Imperial Guard. However, while battle had been raging on the Pratzen, the opposing forces on the northern flank of the battlefield had also clashed violently.

THE BATTLE IN THE NORTH

The Great Cavalry Clash

As part of the grand plan, Bagration held his position in the hills around Posoritz until it became clear that the battle was underway. Then he was to push forward, driving the French before him. Liechtenstein's V Column, composed entirely of cavalry, would occupy the largely open, gently undulating plain, between Bagration and IV Column. In support of both these commands was the Russian Imperial Guard under Grand Duke Constantine. Facing Bagration, some three miles to the west, stood Lannes V Corps and Murat's Cavalry Reserve.

The confusion on the fog-shrouded Pratzen plateau at daybreak ensured that Liechtenstein was late arriving at his appointed position between the villages of Blasowitz and Krug. Due to the disruption caused by marching between elements of III Column, the horsemen arrived in two separate bodies, the Russian regiments arriving first. Bagration was already under way when the Russian cavalry rode up, his left on the villages of Krug and Holubitz while his right extended across the Brünn–Olmütz road to the high ground north-west of Posoritz post house. The Russian cavalry extended this line towards Blasowitz and the Austrians protected the left of the line between Blasowitz and the lower slopes of Staré Vinohrady. Due to the late arrival of Liechtenstein, Grand Duke Constantine had sent forward his battalion of Imperial Guard Jäger to occupy Blasowitz, supported by a Guard Fusilier battalion of the Semenovsky Regiment.

Like Bagration, Lannes too was ordered to delay committing himself until the battle was underway, then move eastwards and push along the Brünn–Olmütz road, getting into a position to prevent any Allied retreat in that direction. He positioned Suchet's Division to the left of the road and Caffarelli's Division to the right. The two battalions of 17ème Légère were detached, the second Battalion garrisoning Santon hill, the anchor of the line, while the 1st Battalion extended to the village of Bosenitz. Murat placed his light cavalry on both flanks and held his two divisions of heavy cavalry in reserve. With these deployments complete this force edged forward sometime between 9.00 and 10.00am. To bring a halt to this forward movement the Russian cavalry, probably just General-Adjutant Uvarov's Brigade (Kharkov Dragoons, Tchernigov Dragoons and Elisabethgrad Hussars) advanced into a storm of fire as Lannes' whole frontline infantry and artillery exploded into action. The attack was repulsed and as the Russians withdrew to re-form, Murat sent Kellermann's light cavalry division (2ème, 4ème, 5ème Hussards and 5ème *Chasseurs à cheval*) to protect the front of Lannes' infantry. Observing this move and unwilling to wait for Uvarov's Brigade to rally the Grand Duke Constantine *Uhlans* charged the light cavalry. Observing this mass of Russian cavalry heading towards him Kellermann retired through Lannes' infantry divisions, leaving the *Uhlans* to confront a deadly rolling fire of close-range musketry all along the line. By the time they had pulled away, the *Uhlans* had suffered heavily and their commander was a prisoner of the French along with 16 other officers. There now followed a confusing sequence of charge and countercharge as the French and Russian cavalry threw themselves hacking and thrusting into a swirling mêlée, before withdrawing, re-forming and charging once more. On the French side there were the cuirassiers and carabiniers of Nansouty and d'Hautpoul, with Kellermann's hussars and *chasseurs à cheval* and Walther's dragoons. Against them rode Uvarov's dragoons and hussars from V Column and the cuirassiers and dragoons of the Army Advance Guard. To the right of Lannes' position, Rivaud's Division of Bernadotte's I Corps appeared in front of Jirzikowitz and immediately attracted the attentions of the Austrian 7. Lothringen *Kürassiere*, which delayed their advance. While these cavalry battles swirled back and forth Bagration made a move on his extreme right, thrusting towards the village of Bosenitz and the stronghold of the Santon beyond. Making a wide arc to the north the Russian 5. Jäger, supported by the Mariupol Hussars and the Khaznenkov Cossacks approached Bosenitz. The outposts of first battalion 17ème Légère were driven back and the village captured. Beyond the village the main body of the first battalion fell back slowly on the Santon, from where artillery fire began to be directed on the pursuing Russians. The Mariupol Hussars made a number of charges against the French battalion but were unable to break them. As they withdrew closer to the Santon the second battalion 17ème was able to add its firepower to the contest. Assailed by these two battalions and the artillery on the Santon, 5. Jäger began to give ground. This retirement quickly degenerated as the second battalion 17ème swept down off the Santon in pursuit with the support of the light cavalry brigades of Milhaud and Treillard who drove off the Mariupol Hussars.

Maréchal Jean Lannes, commander of French V Corps. Lannes occupied a position astride the Brünn–Olmütz road, in direct opposition to Bagration. Both commanders received orders not to commence their forward movements until the battle was under way.

A view of the northern flank of the battlefield, looking east from Santon hill, as it looks today, hardly changed over the intervening years. The old Brünn–Olmütz road, the axis of advance for Lannes and Bagration, is clearly visible running towards the horizon.

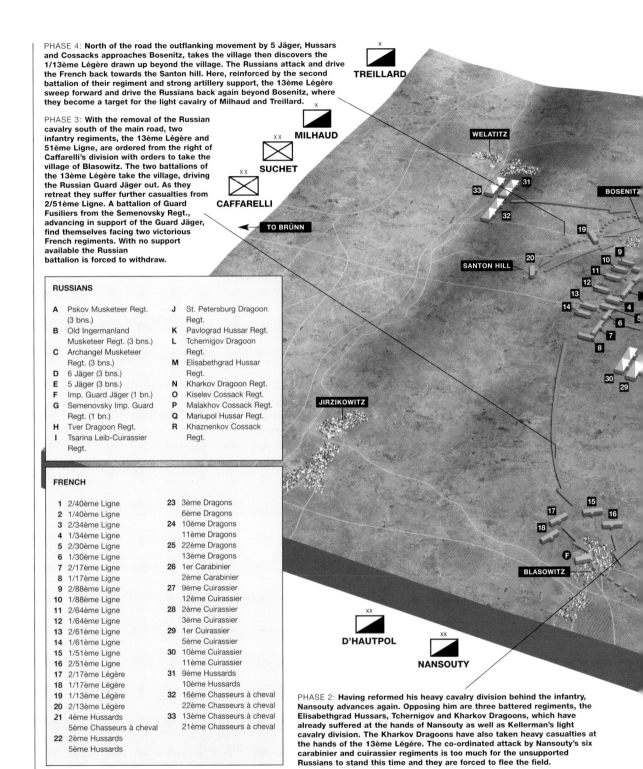

PHASE 4: North of the road the outflanking movement by 5 Jäger, Hussars and Cossacks approaches Bosenitz, takes the village then discovers the 1/13ème Légère drawn up beyond the village. The Russians attack and drive the French back towards the Santon hill. Here, reinforced by the second battalion of their regiment and strong artillery support, the 13ème Légère sweep forward and drive the Russians back again beyond Bosenitz, where they become a target for the light cavalry of Milhaud and Treillard.

PHASE 3: With the removal of the Russian cavalry south of the main road, two infantry regiments, the 13ème Légère and 51ème Ligne, are ordered from the right of Caffarelli's division with orders to take the village of Blasowitz. The two battalions of the 13ème Légère take the village, driving the Russian Guard Jäger out. As they retreat they suffer further casualties from 2/51ème Ligne. A battalion of Guard Fusiliers from the Semenovsky Regt., advancing in support of the Guard Jäger, find themselves facing two victorious French regiments. With no support available the Russian battalion is forced to withdraw.

TREILLARD

MILHAUD

SUCHET

CAFFARELLI

TO BRÜNN

WELATITZ

BOSENITZ

SANTON HILL

JIRZIKOWITZ

BLASOWITZ

D'HAUTPOL

NANSOUTY

RUSSIANS

A Pskov Musketeer Regt. (3 bns.)
B Old Ingermanland Musketeer Regt. (3 bns.)
C Archangel Musketeer Regt. (3 bns.)
D 6 Jäger (3 bns.)
E 5 Jäger (3 bns.)
F Imp. Guard Jäger (1 bn.)
G Semenovsky Imp. Guard Regt. (1 bn.)
H Tver Dragoon Regt.
I Tsarina Leib-Cuirassier Regt.
J St. Petersburg Dragoon Regt.
K Pavlograd Hussar Regt.
L Tchernigov Dragoon Regt.
M Elisabethgrad Hussar Regt.
N Kharkov Dragoon Regt.
O Kiselev Cossack Regt.
P Malakhov Cossack Regt.
Q Mariupol Hussar Regt.
R Khaznenkov Cossack Regt.

FRENCH

1 2/40ème Ligne
2 1/40ème Ligne
3 2/34ème Ligne
4 1/34ème Ligne
5 2/30ème Ligne
6 1/30ème Ligne
7 2/17ème Ligne
8 1/17ème Ligne
9 2/88ème Ligne
10 1/88ème Ligne
11 2/64ème Ligne
12 1/64ème Ligne
13 2/61ème Ligne
14 1/61ème Ligne
15 1/51ème Ligne
16 2/51ème Ligne
17 2/17ème Légère
18 1/17ème Légère
19 1/13ème Légère
20 2/13ème Légère
21 4ème Hussards
    5ème Chasseurs à cheval
22 2ème Hussards
    5ème Hussards
23 3ème Dragons
    6ème Dragons
24 10ème Dragons
    11ème Dragons
25 22ème Dragons
    13ème Dragons
26 1er Carabinier
    2ème Carabinier
27 9ème Cuirassier
    12ème Cuirassier
28 2ème Cuirassier
    3ème Cuirassier
29 1er Cuirassier
    5ème Cuirassier
30 10ème Cuirassier
    11ème Cuirassier
31 9ème Hussards
    10ème Hussards
32 16ème Chasseurs à cheval
    22ème Chasseurs à cheval
33 13ème Chasseurs à cheval
    21ème Chasseurs à cheval

PHASE 2: Having reformed his heavy cavalry division behind the infantry, Nansouty advances again. Opposing him are three battered regiments, the Elisabethgrad Hussars, Tchernigov and Kharkov Dragoons, which have already suffered at the hands of Nansouty as well as Kellerman's light cavalry division. The Kharkov Dragoons have also taken heavy casualties at the hands of the 13ème Légère. The co-ordinated attack by Nansouty's six carabinier and cuirassier regiments is too much for the unsupported Russians to stand this time and they are forced to flee the field.

THE NORTHERN FLANK: LANNES AND MURAT HOLD BAGRATION'S ADVANCE GUARD

2 December 1805, viewed from the south-east, showing the clash along the Brünn–Olmütz road between the Russians of Bagration's Advance Guard and part of Liechtenstein's V Column, and the French of Lannes' V Corps and Murat's Cavalry Reserve

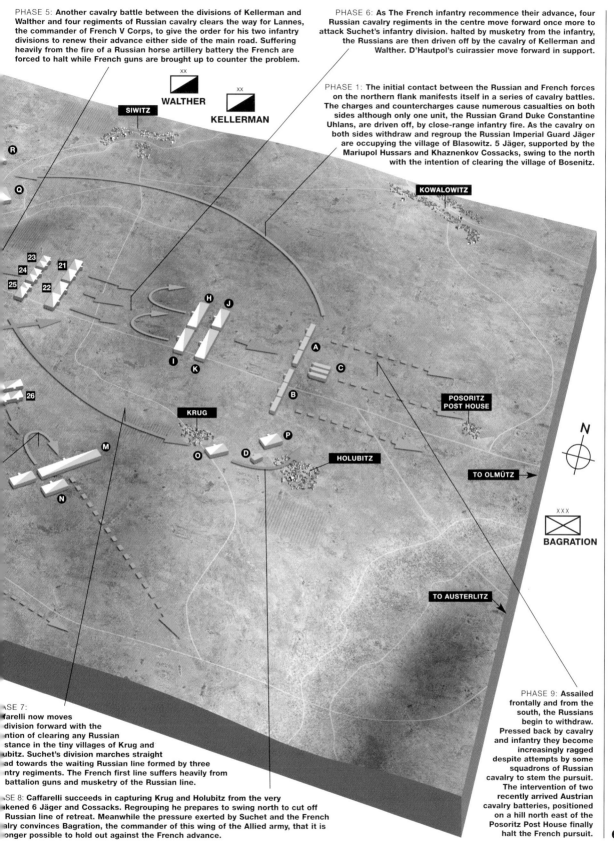

PHASE 5: Another cavalry battle between the divisions of Kellerman and Walther and four regiments of Russian cavalry clears the way for Lannes, the commander of French V Corps, to give the order for his two infantry divisions to renew their advance either side of the main road. Suffering heavily from the fire of a Russian horse artillery battery the French are forced to halt while French guns are brought up to counter the problem.

PHASE 6: As The French infantry recommence their advance, four Russian cavalry regiments in the centre move forward once more to attack Suchet's infantry division. halted by musketry from the infantry, the Russians are then driven off by the cavalry of Kellerman and Walther. D'Hautpol's cuirassier move forward in support.

PHASE 1: The initial contact between the Russian and French forces on the northern flank manifests itself in a series of cavalry battles. The charges and countercharges cause numerous casualties on both sides although only one unit, the Russian Grand Duke Constantine Uhlans, are driven off, by close-range infantry fire. As the cavalry on both sides withdraw and regroup the Russian Imperial Guard Jäger are occupying the village of Blasowitz. 5 Jäger, supported by the Mariupol Hussars and Khaznenkov Cossacks, swing to the north with the intention of clearing the village of Bosenitz.

WALTHER

KELLERMAN

SIWITZ

KOWALOWITZ

KRUG

POSORITZ POST HOUSE

HOLUBITZ

TO OLMÜTZ

N

BAGRATION

TO AUSTERLITZ

\SE 7:
farelli now moves
division forward with the
ntion of clearing any Russian
stance in the tiny villages of Krug and
ubitz. Suchet's division marches straight
ad towards the waiting Russian line formed by three
ntry regiments. The French first line suffers heavily from
battalion guns and musketry of the Russian line.

\SE 8: Caffarelli succeeds in capturing Krug and Holubitz from the very
kened 6 Jäger and Cossacks. Regrouping he prepares to swing north to cut off
Russian line of retreat. Meanwhile the pressure exerted by Suchet and the French
alry convinces Bagration, the commander of this wing of the Allied army, that it is
onger possible to hold out against the French advance.

PHASE 9: Assailed frontally and from the south, the Russians begin to withdraw. Pressed back by cavalry and infantry they become increasingly ragged despite attempts by some squadrons of Russian cavalry to stem the pursuit. The intervention of two recently arrived Austrian cavalry batteries, positioned on a hill north east of the Posoritz Post House finally halt the French pursuit.

65

ABOVE **Général de division Suchet held the extreme left of the French army with his division. Together with Général Caffarelli's Division they were to face attacks by Russian cavalry as the battle developed on the northern flank. (Philip Haythornthwaite)**

RIGHT **Nansouty's cuirassiers advance forward to clash with the Russian cavalry of V Column on the gently rolling ground between Blasowitz and Krug. (Girbal – Sammlung Alfred und Roland Umhey)**

Back closer to the road the cavalry battle had continued, but the repeated charges made by Uvarov's Brigade began to take their toll on the tiring Russian troopers. Having allowed his heavy cavalry a chance to recover behind the infantry, while 13ème Légère on the right of Caffarelli's Division drove off a charge by the Kharkov Dragoons, Murat ordered them out again. With Nansouty's Division to the fore, the rested heavy cavalry formed for battle. As Nansouty arranged his division, with the 1er and 2ème Carabinier and 2ème Cuirassier in the first rank with the 3ème, 9ème and 12ème Cuirassier in the second, to the south the Austrian cavalry were making a last charge. With Vandamme's Division now in control of Staré Vinohrady, Rivaud's Division began to make progress again. Hohenlohe ordered 5. Nassau-Usingen *Kürassiere* forward to forestall this move, however, with Vandamme positioned on their flank the Austrian commander soon retired his cavalry to the east, out of artillery range.

Nansouty's men were now ready and moved forward towards the area between Krug and Blasowitz where Uvarov's exhausted cavalry was re-forming. The Russians gamely advanced towards the approaching carabiniers and cuirassiers but this time the result was decisive and

Uvarov's men fell back to the high ground between the Raussnitz stream and the Austerlitz road. Here they found the Tsar and what remained of his retinue.

Lannes and Murat Secure the North

A large gap had now opened between the Allied right and centre, occupied only by the battalion of Russian Guard Jäger in Blasowitz, seriously weakening Bagration's position. Bagration had received no fresh orders since the battle began and was unaware of the result of the fighting elsewhere. With the Allied cavalry threat now removed on his right, Lannes ordered his infantry forward, detailing 13ème Légère and 51ème Ligne to wrest Blasowitz from the Jäger. Although outnumbered, the Russian defenders managed to rebuff an attack by the 13ème but when they assaulted a second time in strength the isolated Jäger exited from the village only to run into the fire of a battalion of the 51ème. The Jäger headed eastwards to safety, followed quickly by the 500 men of the Guard Fusilier battalion of the Semenovsky Regiment, who, positioned behind Blasowitz, found themselves the new target for these four French battalions. Now the whole plain south of the Brünn–Olmütz road as well as the Pratzen plateau was under French control.

Lannes and Murat pressed forward against Bagration. A heavy exchange of artillery fire took place and although the Russian line could not be broken, with pressure from front and left, it gradually began to give ground. The Russians protected their retreat by a number of self-sacrificing unco-ordinated cavalry charges by those regiments still clinging to the main body. Bagration fell back beyond the important junction on the Brünn–Olmütz road, where a road branched off to Austerlitz, and re-formed his men on the high ground around the village of Welleschowitz. The French pressure continued and it looked as though Bagration would be pushed back along the Olmütz road, away from the rest of the army, when help arrived. Rushing along the road from Olmütz two batteries of Austrian guns commanded by Major Frierenberger arrived and quickly deployed on high ground north of

TOP **A view of Santon hill from the outskirts of the village of Bosenitz. The Russian 5. Jäger captured the village but were unable to make any further progress in the face of opposition from the French 17éme Ligne and artillery positioned on the summit.**

ABOVE **An officer of the French 5ème Hussards, part of Kellermann's light cavalry division. The 5ème Hussards were heavily involved in the cavalry battles that developed in the open country on the northern flank. (Philip Haythornthwaite)**

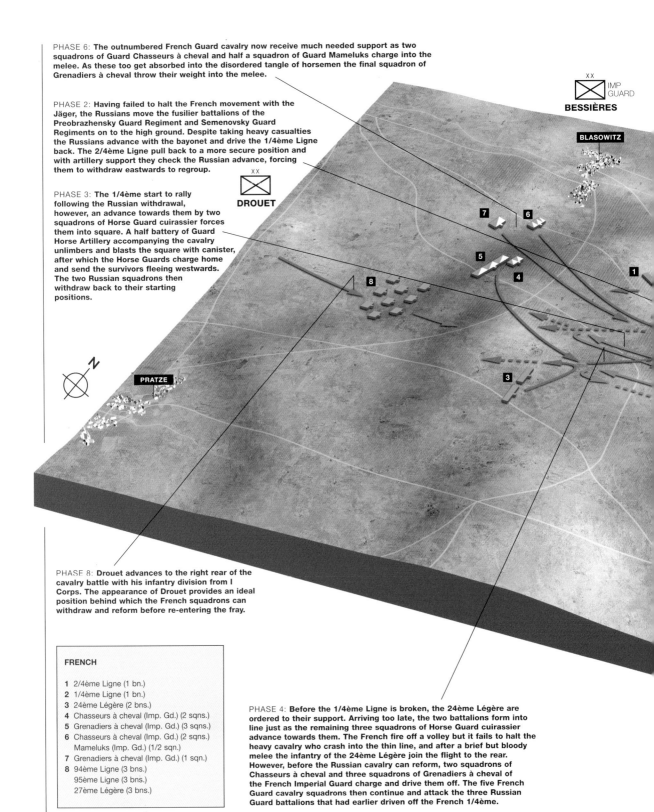

PHASE 6: **The outnumbered French Guard cavalry now receive much needed support as two squadrons of Guard Chasseurs à cheval and half a squadron of Guard Mameluks charge into the melee. As these too get absorbed into the disordered tangle of horsemen the final squadron of Grenadiers à cheval throw their weight into the melee.**

PHASE 2: **Having failed to halt the French movement with the Jäger, the Russians move the fusilier battalions of the Preobrazhensky Guard Regiment and Semenovsky Guard Regiments on to the high ground. Despite taking heavy casualties the Russians advance with the bayonet and drive the 1/4ème Ligne back. The 2/4ème Ligne pull back to a more secure position and with artillery support they check the Russian advance, forcing them to withdraw eastwards to regroup.**

PHASE 3: **The 1/4ème start to rally following the Russian withdrawal, however, an advance towards them by two squadrons of Horse Guard cuirassier forces them into square. A half battery of Guard Horse Artillery accompanying the cavalry unlimbers and blasts the square with canister, after which the Horse Guards charge home and send the survivors fleeing westwards. The two Russian squadrons then withdraw back to their starting positions.**

x x
BESSIÈRES IMP GUARD

BLASOWITZ

x x
DROUET

7   **6**

5   **1**

4

8

3

PRATZE

PHASE 8: **Drouet advances to the right rear of the cavalry battle with his infantry division from I Corps. The appearance of Drouet provides an ideal position behind which the French squadrons can withdraw and reform before re-entering the fray.**

FRENCH

1 2/4ème Ligne (1 bn.)
2 1/4ème Ligne (1 bn.)
3 24ème Légère (2 bns.)
4 Chasseurs à cheval (Imp. Gd.) (2 sqns.)
5 Grenadiers à cheval (Imp. Gd.) (3 sqns.)
6 Chasseurs à cheval (Imp. Gd.) (2 sqns.)
   Mameluks (Imp. Gd.) (1/2 sqn.)
7 Grenadiers à cheval (Imp. Gd.) (1 sqn.)
8 94ème Ligne (3 bns.)
   95ème Ligne (3 bns.)
   27ème Légère (3 bns.)

PHASE 4: **Before the 1/4ème Ligne is broken, the 24ème Légère are ordered to their support. Arriving too late, the two battalions form into line just as the remaining three squadrons of Horse Guard cuirassier advance towards them. The French fire off a volley but it fails to halt the heavy cavalry who crash into the thin line, and after a brief but bloody melee the infantry of the 24ème Légère join the flight to the rear. However, before the Russian cavalry can reform, two squadrons of Chasseurs à cheval and three squadrons of Grenadiers à cheval of the French Imperial Guard charge and drive them off. The five French Guard cavalry squadrons then continue and attack the three Russian Guard battalions that had earlier driven off the French 1/4ème.**

ATTACK OF THE RUSSIAN IMPERIAL GUARD
2 December 1805, viewed from the south-east, showing the defeat of the attack of the Russian Imperial Guard

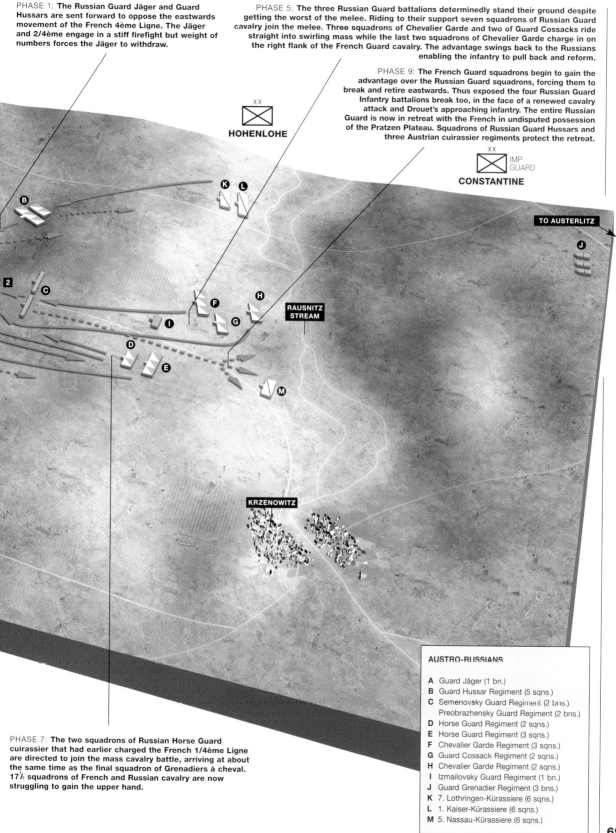

PHASE 1: The Russian Guard Jäger and Guard Hussars are sent forward to oppose the eastwards movement of the French 4ème Ligne. The Jäger and 2/4ème engage in a stiff firefight but weight of numbers forces the Jäger to withdraw.

PHASE 5: The three Russian Guard battalions determinedly stand their ground despite getting the worst of the melee. Riding to their support seven squadrons of Russian Guard cavalry join the melee. Three squadrons of Chevalier Garde and two of Guard Cossacks ride straight into swirling mass while the last two squadrons of Chevalier Garde charge in on the right flank of the French Guard cavalry. The advantage swings back to the Russians enabling the infantry to pull back and reform.

PHASE 9: The French Guard squadrons begin to gain the advantage over the Russian Guard squadrons, forcing them to break and retire eastwards. Thus exposed the four Russian Guard Infantry battalions break too, in the face of a renewed cavalry attack and Drouet's approaching infantry. The entire Russian Guard is now in retreat with the French in undisputed possession of the Pratzen Plateau. Squadrons of Russian Guard Hussars and three Austrian cuirassier regiments protect the retreat.

x x
HOHENLOHE

x x   IMP
GUARD
CONSTANTINE

TO AUSTERLITZ

**RAUSNITZ
STREAM**

KRZENOWITZ

PHASE 7: The two squadrons of Russian Horse Guard cuirassier that had earlier charged the French 1/4ème Ligne are directed to join the mass cavalry battle, arriving at about the same time as the final squadron of Grenadiers à cheval. 17½ squadrons of French and Russian cavalry are now struggling to gain the upper hand.

AUSTRO-RUSSIANS

A Guard Jäger (1 bn.)
B Guard Hussar Regiment (5 sqns.)
C Semenovsky Guard Regiment (2 bns.)
  Preobrazhensky Guard Regiment (2 bns.)
D Horse Guard Regiment (2 sqns.)
E Horse Guard Regiment (3 sqns.)
F Chevalier Garde Regiment (3 sqns.)
G Guard Cossack Regiment (2 sqns.)
H Chevalier Garde Regiment (2 sqns.)
I Izmailovsky Guard Regiment (1 bn.)
J Guard Grenadier Regiment (3 bns.)
K 7. Lothringen-Kürassiere (6 sqns.)
L 1. Kaiser-Kürassiere (6 sqns.)
M 5. Nassau-Kürassiere (6 sqns.)

69

Welleschowitz. The French line had now reached the Posoritz post house but had no response to the accurate fire of these 12 guns. The French batteries pulled back, losing some guns in the process; the infantry halted. The French advance in the north had run its course.

THE ATTACK OF THE RUSSIAN IMPERIAL GUARD

While the battle raged in the north, fighting had again flared up on the Pratzen plateau. During the morning, Grand Duke Constantine moved up to the east of Blasowitz with the Russian Imperial Guard, forming his illustrious command in three lines. The three battalions that formed the Guard Grenadier Regiment were still a long way behind. Having pushed the Jäger forward into Blasowitz and supported them with a battalion of Guard Fusiliers of the Semenovsky Regiment, Constantine received a request from Miloradovich for help on the Pratzen plateau. In response he despatched a battalion of Guard Fusiliers from the Izmailovsky Regiment, who arrived as the tide of Austrian and Russian refugees fleeing from Vandamme's assault on Staré Vinohrady swept passed and engulfed them. Recognising the exposed nature of his position Constantine ordered the Imperial Guard back to a position behind the Raussnitz stream, where he hoped to combine with rallied elements of IV Column. The Guard Jäger and Fusiliers of the Semenovsky Regiment previously driven away from Blasowitz rejoined the main body of the Guard. Hohenlohe formed his *kürassiere* to their rear, protecting the flanks.

Vandamme, on the high ground had a reasonably clear view of this realignment by the Allies and was in the process of reorganising his division, which had been disrupted by the fight for Staré Vinohrady. In

TOP **Lannes' attack presses forward beyond the village of Bosenitz. The Russians are holding their line just to the west of Krug and Holubitz. (Tapetenmuseum, Kassel – Sammlung Alfred und Roland Umhey)**

ABOVE **Repeated attacks by the French cavalry on Bagration's command as it pulled back failed to break its resistance. Here a Russian grenadier, wearing the 1805 shako, faces an attack by the French 4ème Hussards. (Girbal – Sammlung Alfred und Roland Umhey)**

LEFT **The leading squadron of Horse Guards of the Russian Imperial Guard charge towards the hastily formed square of the first battalion of the French 4ème Ligne. (Artillery Museum, St. Petersburg – Sammlung Alfred und Roland Umhey)**

BELOW, LEFT **Soldiers of the French 4ème Ligne repel the first Russian Guard squadron, but the second squadron charged home and sent the battalion into headlong retreat. (Girbal – Sammlung Alfred und Roland Umhey)**

OVERLEAF
THE CHARGE OF THE RUSSIAN IMPERIAL GUARD.
With Vandamme's division occupying the Staré Vinohrady at the northern end of the Pratzen plateau, Grand Duke Constantine, commander of the Russian Imperial Guard, was determined to prevent them pressing on further. An infantry assault by the Guard Fusiliers met with initial success before recoiling in the face of concentrated French artillery fire and musketry. As the first battalion of the 4ème Ligne recovered from the Russian attack the cavalry of the Russian Imperial Guard moved up. The French battalion rapidly formed square, but as they awaited the inevitable onslaught Russian guns opened fire on the compact formation. Seizing the moment Constantine ordered two squadrons of the Horse Guards to charge. The leading squadron, receiving a close range volley and veered away but the second squadron charged home and slashed their way into the disintegrating square. The prized Eagle of the battalion drew Russians like moths to a candle. Defended desperately by Sergeant Major Saint-Cyr, the Guard cavalry eventually hacked the Eagle from him, the blood-soaked NCO slumping to the ground having sustained numerous cuts to his arms and head. (Christa Hook)

preparation for a further advance he ordered the two battalions of 4ème Ligne to move into the vineyards that lay on the northern slopes of Staré Vinohrady to anchor his line. In a show of force designed to prevent the French descending from the plateau, Constantine moved back across the Raussnitz stream with his reordered command. The Jäger, who appear to have recovered quickly from their defeat at Blasowitz, were protecting the northern flank of the formation with the Guard Hussars when they received an order to oppose this move by the 4ème Ligne. The Jäger moved into the vineyard where a firefight broke out with the second battalion of the French regiment. With the stakes of the vineyard running on an east–west line the Guard Hussars, who had

With the Russians gradually gaining the upper hand Napoleon ordered his remaining two squadrons of *Chasseurs à cheval* and a half squadron of Mameluks into the mêlée. In the illustrations the leading Mameluks clash with the *Chevalier Garde.* (Hourtoulle – Sammlung Alfred und Roland Umhey)

approached from the north hung back in support outside the vineyard. As soon as this engagement was under way Constantine sent forward four battalions of Guard Fusiliers of the Semenovsky and Preobrazhensky Regiments up the gentle slope through the vineyard. So determined were these men to get to grips with the French that discipline was lost and they covered the last 300 paces to the French line at a run. Despite the concentrated fire from the first Battalion 4ème Ligne, their breathlessness and the disruption to their formations caused by moving through the vincyard the Russian Guardsmen smashed into the French battalion at the point of the bayonet and broke their line. As the attack rolled forward, the second battalion, who had driven back the Guard Jäger, retired on an artillery battery. The Russians continued in some disorder towards this second line, but a destructive concentration of artillery fire and musketry prevented them from reaching it. Bloodied and battered they retired to the edge of the vineyard and regrouped.

With the recall of the Russian Guardsmen the first battalion of 4ème Ligne was able to re-form and had just completed their reorganisation when a large force of Russian cavalry, 17 squadrons of the Russian Imperial Guard, advanced towards them. The French battalion changed formation to square amongst the battered vines, and the 24ème Légère were ordered up to support them, but before they could respond the Russians unlimbered half a battery of Guard Horse Artillery and commenced blasting the compact formation. Considering the French square suitably weakened, the Horse Guards prepared to charge. With Grand Duke Constantine at their head and with his cry 'For God, the Tsar and Russia!' inspiring them, two squadrons of the regiment closed on the square. The

first squadron, advancing along the line of the vines, almost reached the French position when a volley crashed out with such power that the Russian horsemen veered away. However, the second squadron escaped this menace and crashed into the square, laying about them left and right, hacking and thrusting with their swords. The desperate, maddened souls that gathered about the Eagle as the battalion disintegrated defended it with their lives, but it was cut from them and carried away – the sole trophy taken by the Allies to balance against the many captured by the French.

As the two Russian squadrons retired to their original position to rally, the breathless 24ème Légère arrived, entered the vineyard and formed a line facing the Russian position. Observing their arrival the three remaining squadrons of the Horse Guard spurred forward and charged this blue line. The weight of the charge carried the horsemen through the French infantry, breaking the formation and throwing it into confusion. The 24ème followed their comrades from the 4ème Ligne. Napoleon and his entourage were making their way up to the high point of Staré Vinohrady as the mass of fleeing men from 4ème flowed passed. Unable to rally them, Napoleon recognised the danger and ordered Marshal Bessières, commander of the French Imperial Guard, to attack the Russian cavalry. Leading with two squadrons of the Guard *Chasseurs à cheval* supported by three squadrons of Guard *Grenadiers à cheval* and two batteries of horse artillery, the French slammed into the ranks of the Russian Guard squadrons, now disorganised by their charge and mêlée with the infantry, and drove them off. The impetus of the charge carried the French cavalry on through the vineyard and into the ranks of the Russian Guard Fusilier battalions of the Semenovsky and Preobrazhensky Regiments. Despite

The final squadron of the *Grenadiers à cheval* charge into the mêlée. The Russians also fed in their last two squadrons and, although outnumbered, the greater discipline of the French began to take its toll. (Private Collection, photo A. Umhey)

the momentum of the attack the infantry held firm and battled on, with a battalion of the Izmailovsky Guard Fusiliers in support; musket and bayonet against sword, sabre and pistol. While this combat hung in the balance Constantine threw in his last fresh reserves – five squadrons of the *Chevalier Garde* and two squadrons of Guard Cossacks. These fresh arrivals swung the struggle in favour of the Russians. To redress this, Napoleon, who was watching the combat unfold, ordered the last squadrons of his Guard into the struggling mass. Commanded by General Rapp, one of Napoleon's Aides-de-Camp, the last two squadrons of *Chasseurs à cheval* and the half squadron of Mameluks of the Guard sliced their way into the swirling mêlée but their momentum was slowed by the sheer mass of men and horses. Napoleon ordered his last squadron, from the *Grenadiers à cheval*, to join the slaughter, and as they did so Constantine sent in the two squadrons of Horse Guards that had earlier successfully charged the 4ème Ligne. So confused had the action become that the Russian Guard Fusiliers no longer felt able to fire into the mass for fear of hitting their own cavalry.

To the west of this struggling mass of infantry and cavalry, General Drouet moved up with his division. Part of Bernadotte's I Corps, Drouet's timely arrival provided a refuge for the tiring French Imperial Guard cavalry. Behind the massed ranks of these nine battalions, drawn up in three lines, the cavalry regrouped and returned to the action. The Russian Guard cavalry outnumbered those of the French Guard but the discipline and control of the French horsemen was greater than that of their opponents and gradually they began to break up the Russian squadrons, who retired to the rear. With their proud cavalry beaten, the Guard Fusiliers extricated themselves as best they could from the blood-soaked maelstrom that had descended upon them and made good their retreat towards Krzenowitz. Some squadrons of the Russian Guard Hussars hovering on the northern flank of the battle prevented the French cavalry pursuing the Russian infantry with determination.

Hohenlohe's three regiments of Austrian heavy cavalry guarding the approaches to Krzenowitz gave the retreating troops the support they needed to avoid a rout. The long awaited appearance of the three battalions of the Russian Imperial Guard Grenadiers also helped stabilize the situation.

The victory already belonged to Napoleon. The Allied centre had been broken and the French forces on the northern flank were gradually pushing the Russians back. The epic battle for the Pratzen and the determined encounter on the northern flank had been played out while Davout and Legrand were manfully holding back the Allied left wing in the Goldbach valley. It was now a question of the scale of the victory. Leaving Bernadotte to hold the northern end of the Pratzen plateau with Drouet's Division, Napoleon turned the rest of his available forces to the south in an attempt to surround and crush Buxhöwden's command.

SOULT ATTACKS THE ALLIED LEFT

Following the destruction of Allied IV Column on the Pratzen plateau, Kutuzov sent word to Buxhöwden advising him to break off the action on the Goldbach and retire. Whether he received these orders or did not comprehend the seriousness of the situation on the plateau is unclear. What is certain is that when the French appeared on the summit of the plateau and prepared to march against his rear, the left wing of the army was still engaged in the long drawn out fight around Sokolnitz.

With the threat from the Russian Imperial Guard removed, Napoleon ordered the battle-weary divisions of St. Hilaire and Vandamme to march to the southern end of Pratzen plateau. Behind them followed the Imperial Guard and the Reserve Grenadier Division. It was probably about 2.00pm. St. Hilaire's Division was in position first, on the edge of the plateau looking down on the village of Sokolnitz and the Russian rear, occupying the position vacated by Langeron's II Column at dawn that morning. Vandamme needed time to re-form his two brigades that had been in action against the Russian Guard but his third, Candras'

View from the position occupied by St.Hilaire's Division on the Pratzen plateau overlooking Sokolnitz (on right of photo). Langeron and Prebyshevsky's Columns were still involved in the battle for the control of the village when St.Hilaire's men marched against their rear.

Brigade, hastened onwards and formed behind St. Hilaire in support. In preparation for this final onslaught Legrand formed the three brigades of his division of IV Corps on St. Hilaire's right flank, extending the line to the north of Sokolnitz. Fighting flared up again in Sokolnitz and around the castle as Davout continued his audacious attacks designed to tie down the Allied left wing. Just at this moment Langeron and Prebyshevsky, already concerned by their dwindling supplies of ammunition, saw St. Hilaire begin his descent from the plateau towards their rear. It was clear to them both that the battle was lost, it was now up to them to extricate their men as best they could. Langeron, who started the battle with 17 battalions, had bled away eight in the attack against St. Hilaire on the Pratzeberg. Managing to get orders to five of his battalions (three battalions of Viborg Musketeers and two battalions of 8. Jäger) Langeron marched south, away from the menacing St. Hilaire. His other four battalions, heavily engaged with Friant's men around Sokolnitz and the castle, could not fight their way out in time. After the initial battles for control of Sokolnitz, Prebyshevsky had extended his command so that it defended the walled pheasantry north of Sokolnitz as well as the castle. The Galicia and Butyrsk Musketeer Regiments occupied the pheasantry with the heavily depleted Narva, Azov and Podolia Musketeer Regiments in reserve to the east. In an effort to evade capture, Prebyshevsky ordered his command to attempt a break-out to the north, where if the overall Allied plan had been successful he hoped to find IV Column. Such was the breakdown in communications caused by the French assault on the Pratzen plateau that he was unaware that IV Column had been defeated. It was a brave effort but it was doomed. Prebyshevsky continued to exert some control over his increasingly desperate men as far as the Kobelnitz ponds but by then the pressure was becoming irresistable. The sheer volume of French fire from the encircling units of St. Hilaire, Legrand and Oudinot and the inability to replenish his own supplies led to the disintegration of III Column. Prebyshevsky and a number of senior officers became prisoners, along with a great number of his men. In the meantime, Sokolnitz and the castle were once more in French hands, the Russian defenders were overwhelmed and driven out, having made a desperate stand. The fighting had been vicious and bloody. The main street of the village was described as being, ' … entirely covered with the dead and wounded of both sides. The corpses were heaped up on one another.' Another participant reflected that the battle for supremacy of this devastated collection of ruined buildings had been 'slaughter', individual Russians fighting on when all around them were dead.

THE FLIGHT ACROSS THE ICE

While the dramatic French descent from the plateau fell upon the rear of II and III Columns, Kienmayer and Dokhturov, on the extreme left of the Allied line, still had time to organise their retreat. Buxhöwden moved off first, initially intending to move eastwards and form a junction with IV Column, although he did not know exactly where he would find it. Langeron's remnants of II Column followed with the main body of I Column behind. Kienmayer and Dokhturov formed a rearguard from Kienmayer's advance guard of I Corps augmented by a

battalion of 7. Jäger. These were the soldiers that had confidently fired the first shots in anger early that morning, now they were protecting the retreat of a defeated army.

Once this body was on the move the rearguard pulled back from the village of Telnitz on to the high ground to the east, still covering the retreat. On Kienmayer's orders GM Nostitz headed south with his cavalry brigade, comprising mainly 4. Hessen-Homburg Husaren, leading the way for the gradual retirement of the rearguard. His orders were to hold a position on high ground between Satschan and Ottnitz to prevent any French attempt to cut off the rearguard. Following the edge of the frozen Satschan pond he turned eastwards and crossed a narrow causeway separating it from Menitz pond. Behind Nostitz marched the infantry of the rearguard. This movement attracted the attention of French artillery close to Telnitz. Their accurate fire caused an ammunition wagon to explode on the causeway, forcing some guns to be abandoned and the troops following to detour across the ice of the Menitz pond, which fortunately was strong enough to bear the weight.

Buxhöwden had reached the vicinity of Augezd without meeting any opposition. Some French infantry had begun to appear on the heights above out of musket range and a Russian battery had unlimbered and opened fire on them. There was a narrow defile between the village and the Satschan pond, so to secure the line of retreat 8. Jäger from II Column occupied the houses and gardens as the leading elements filed slowly past. However, the Frenchmen gathering on the high ground, Vandamme's brigades that had experienced such fearsome fighting on Staré Vinohrady, were finally arriving in strength. The first to descend was first Battalion 28ème Ligne, being quickly hustled down the slope to cut the road that ran east from Augezd. With the division's artillery now in a position to lend support and the remaining regiments formed, Vandamme ordered the battalions of 4ème Ligne, 24ème Légère and second Battalion 28ème Ligne to sweep down and take Augezd. The torrent engulfed 8. Jäger and the Russian gunners who

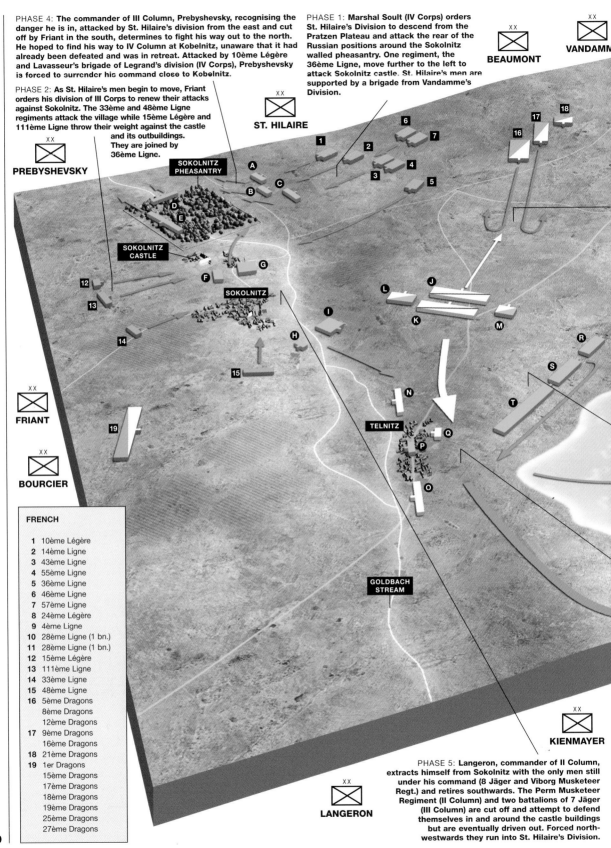

PHASE 4: The commander of III Column, Prebyshevsky, recognising the danger he is in, attacked by St. Hilaire's division from the east and cut off by Friant in the south, determines to fight his way out to the north. He hoped to find his way to IV Column at Kobelnitz, unaware that it had already been defeated and was in retreat. Attacked by 10ème Légère and Lavasseur's brigade of Legrand's division (IV Corps), Prebyshevsky is forced to surrender his command close to Kobelnitz.

PHASE 2: As St. Hilaire's men begin to move, Friant orders his division of III Corps to renew their attacks against Sokolnitz. The 33ème and 48ème Ligne regiments attack the village while 15ème Légère and 111ème Ligne throw their weight against the castle and its outbuildings. They are joined by 36ème Ligne.

PHASE 1: Marshal Soult (IV Corps) orders St. Hilaire's Division to descend from the Pratzen Plateau and attack the rear of the Russian positions around the Sokolnitz walled pheasantry. One regiment, the 36ème Ligne, move further to the left to attack Sokolnitz castle. St. Hilaire's men are supported by a brigade from Vandamme's Division.

BEAUMONT

VANDAMME

ST. HILAIRE

PREBYSHEVSKY

SOKOLNITZ PHEASANTRY

SOKOLNITZ CASTLE

SOKOLNITZ

FRIANT

BOURCIER

TELNITZ

GOLDBACH STREAM

KIENMAYER

LANGERON

PHASE 5: Langeron, commander of II Column, extracts himself from Sokolnitz with the only men still under his command (8 Jäger and Viborg Musketeer Regt.) and retires southwards. The Perm Musketeer Regiment (II Column) and two battalions of 7 Jäger (III Column) are cut off and attempt to defend themselves in and around the castle buildings but are eventually driven out. Forced north-westwards they run into St. Hilaire's Division.

FRENCH

1	10ème Légère
2	14ème Ligne
3	43ème Ligne
4	55ème Ligne
5	36ème Ligne
6	46ème Ligne
7	57ème Ligne
8	24ème Légère
9	4ème Ligne
10	28ème Ligne (1 bn.)
11	28ème Ligne (1 bn.)
12	15ème Légère
13	111ème Ligne
14	33ème Ligne
15	48ème Ligne
16	5ème Dragons
	8ème Dragons
	12ème Dragons
17	9ème Dragons
	16ème Dragons
18	21ème Dragons
19	1er Dragons
	15ème Dragons
	17ème Dragons
	18ème Dragons
	19ème Dragons
	25ème Dragons
	27ème Dragons

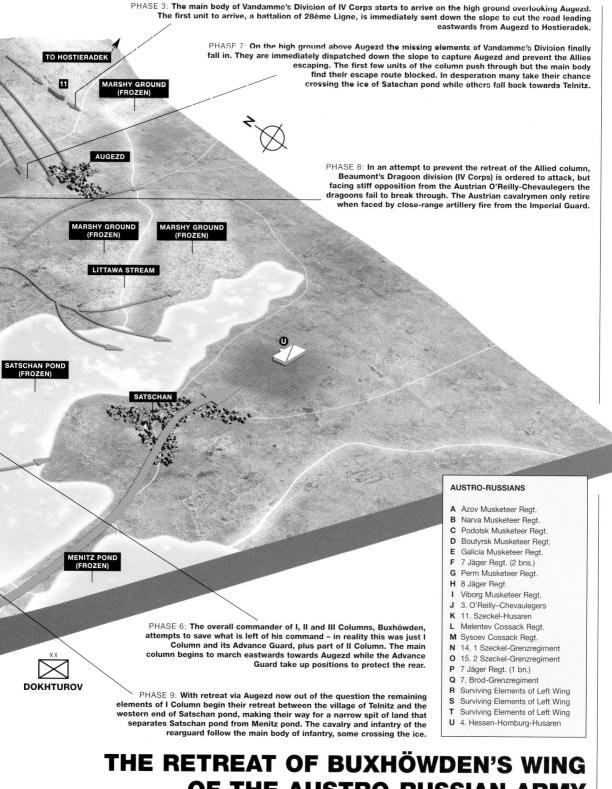

PHASE 3: The main body of Vandamme's Division of IV Corps starts to arrive on the high ground overlooking Augezd. The first unit to arrive, a battalion of 28ème Ligne, is immediately sent down the slope to cut the road leading eastwards from Augezd to Hostieradek.

PHASE 7: On the high ground above Augezd the missing elements of Vandamme's Division finally fall in. They are immediately dispatched down the slope to capture Augezd and prevent the Allies escaping. The first few units of the column push through but the main body find their escape route blocked. In desperation many take their chance crossing the ice of Satschan pond while others fall back towards Telnitz.

PHASE 8: In an attempt to prevent the retreat of the Allied column, Beaumont's Dragoon division (IV Corps) is ordered to attack, but facing stiff opposition from the Austrian O'Reilly-Chevaulegers the dragoons fail to break through. The Austrian cavalrymen only retire when faced by close-range artillery fire from the Imperial Guard.

TO HOSTIERADEK

11

MARSHY GROUND (FROZEN)

AUGEZD

MARSHY GROUND (FROZEN)

MARSHY GROUND (FROZEN)

LITTAWA STREAM

SATSCHAN POND (FROZEN)

SATSCHAN

MENITZ POND (FROZEN)

DOKHTUROV

PHASE 6: The overall commander of I, II and III Columns, Buxhöwden, attempts to save what is left of his command – in reality this was just I Column and its Advance Guard, plus part of II Column. The main column begins to march eastwards towards Augezd while the Advance Guard take up positions to protect the rear.

PHASE 9: With retreat via Augezd now out of the question the remaining elements of I Column begin their retreat between the village of Telnitz and the western end of Satschan pond, making their way for a narrow spit of land that separates Satschan pond from Menitz pond. The cavalry and infantry of the rearguard follow the main body of infantry, some crossing the ice.

AUSTRO-RUSSIANS

A Azov Musketeer Regt.
B Narva Musketeer Regt.
C Podolsk Musketeer Regt.
D Boutyrsk Musketeer Regt.
E Galicia Musketeer Regt.
F 7 Jäger Regt. (2 bns.)
G Perm Musketeer Regt.
H 8 Jäger Regt.
I Viborg Musketeer Regt.
J 3. O'Reilly–Chevaulegers
K 11. Szeckel-Husaren
L Melentev Cossack Regt.
M Sysoev Cossack Regt.
N 14. 1 Szeckel-Grenzregiment
O 15. 2 Szeckel-Grenzregiment
P 7 Jäger Regt. (1 bn.)
Q 7. Brod-Grenzregiment
R Surviving Elements of Left Wing
S Surviving Elements of Left Wing
T Surviving Elements of Left Wing
U 4. Hessen-Homburg-Husaren

THE RETREAT OF BUXHÖWDEN'S WING OF THE AUSTRO-RUSSIAN ARMY

2 December 1805, 2.00pm–4.00pm, viewed from the south-west showing the retreat of the Allied left wing and the flight across the frozen ponds.

Napoleon and his staff at the Chapel of St. Antonin at the southern end of the Pratzen plateau, overlooking the village of Augezd. From here Napoleon observed his cavalry fail in their attempt to destroy the Allied rearguard. (Girbal – Sammlung Alfred und Roland Umhey)

defended their pieces to the last. Retreat past Augezd was now out of the question. Only a few groups had managed to get beyond Augezd before the route was blocked. Those leading the following section, headed by Buxhöwden and his staff, veered off southwards and headed for a narrow wooden bridge that crossed the ponds. Buxhöwden made it safely to the other side but the heavy traffic that followed smashed through the planking, denying this escape route to the rest of the column. With limited options now available a mass of fugitives began to slither across the ice. The weight of men, horses and limbers was too much for the ice to bear and inevitably it gave way, dumping the soldiers into the icy blackness of the pond. Seeing the confusion, the French artillery opened on this struggling target. Luckily for the Russians the water was not deep and a number staggered through to the safety of the far bank. Probably about 200 men died in the pond, their bodies dragged from the water by comrades and Vandamme's men. Many more

An Austrian cavalry battery and the O'Reilly *Chevaulegers* prevented Beaumont's dragoon division from breaking through to the retreating Allied infantry. It was only after a battery of Guard artillery opened on them that the *Chevaulegers* finally withdrew.

became prisoners. The rearmost sections of the column, having seen the horror develop ahead, turned back towards Telnitz where the rearguard was still holding on.

The rearguard cavalry formed a protective screen behind which the perplexed infantry restored order before marching to the causeway between Satschan and Menitz ponds, the only escape route remaining open. Some made a dash across the ice, which held firm. The Austrian

Napoleon touring the battlefield after the fighting had ended. He regularly stopped and talked with the wounded. In this illustration he is receiving Allied officer prisoners and an array of captured trophies. (Château de Grosbois – Sammlung Alfred und Roland Umhey)

cavalry was drawn up in two lines, 3. O'Reilly *Chevaulegers* in front under the command of GM Stutterheim, with 11. Szeckel Husaren, led by GM Moritz Liechtenstein, behind. The Sysoev and Melentev Cossacks hovered on their flanks and a Russian infantry unit still hung on around Telnitz. Determined to prevent any more Allied troops escaping, Beaumont's 3ème Dragoon Division, attached to IV Corps, was ordered to break through the cavalry rearguard. Opposed by the O'Reilly *Chevaulegers* and some highly accurate fire by an Austrian cavalry battery the dragoons failed. Napoleon grew angry as he watched the cavalry fail to prevent the Russian infantry continuing their slow deliberate march to safety. The O'Reilly *Chevaulegers* held firm until artillery fire from a battery of Guard Artillery inflicted heavy casualties forcing them to retreat, but they had succeeded in gaining enough time for all the remaining survivors of I Column to escape capture. The Szeckel Husaren had stood firmly in support of the *chevaulegers* throughout their attacks on the dragoons despite galling artillery fire. Now the rearguard headed for the causeway and safety, some venturing to make their own escape across the ice. It was now around 4.00pm, the winter's sky was darkening and an icy rain fell on victor and vanquished alike. There was no further French pursuit. The battle of Austerlitz was over.

Napoleon watched the last remnants of the Austro-Russian army melt away into the gathering gloom. Accompanied by Berthier and Soult he rode slowly down from the slopes of the Pratzen plateau towards the Satschan pond, moving through the ranks of his victorious soldiers. Later he journeyed north, stopping regularly to offer comfort to wounded soldiers before reaching the Posoritz post house, where he slept that night, no doubt reflecting, with his great sense of theatre, that this day was the first anniversary of his coronation as Emperor. Here he wrote his proclamation to the army, opening with the line, 'Soldiers, I am pleased with you,' it went on to acknowledge the enormity of the army's achievement. In conclusion he ended with the words, 'My people will greet you with joy, and it will be enough for you to say, "I was at the Battle of Austerlitz", and they will reply "There stands a hero!"'

PAGES 84–85
THE ALLIED RETREAT ACROSS THE SATSCHAN PONDS
With the battle clearly lost, those Allies still able to extricate themselves headed for the only open escape route between the southern end of the Pratzen plateau and the frozen Satschan pond. The French quickly blocked this avenue of escape through Augezd, and forced south, the leading units veered towards a narrow wooden bridge over the ice. This soon collapsed under the weight of the panicked traffic, however, and left with no alternative the Allies began to venture on to the ice and make their way tentatively across, wagons and artillery limbers soon joining the flight. Unable to bear this weight the ice began to crack then break. Seeing this, French artillery now drawn up overlooking the village of Augezd opened fire on the frozen pond adding to the confusion. However, the pond was shallow and few men drowned despite Napoleon's extraordinary claims of 20,000 dead. Rather than risk their lives on the ice, those still able turned back and made good their escape around the south side of the Satschan pond protected by a resolute rearguard. (Christa Hook)

THE AFTERMATH

Through the night of 2/3 December the widely separated elements of the Allied army retreated and eventually gathered together at Czeitsch on the road leading to Hungary. In the early hours of the morning Prince Johann Liechtenstein arrived at Napoleon's headquarters to arrange a meeting between Emperor Francis and Napoleon. The army continued to withdraw in appalling weather, unmolested by the French, who mistakenly believed the Allies were retiring on the Olmütz road. It was only after Napoleon moved his headquarters to Austerlitz that he discovered the error and recalled Murat and Lannes. On 4 December the Allies began to cross the March River at Holíc. The meeting between Napoleon and Francis took place that day and an armistice was agreed, coming into effect the following day. The French army finally closed on the Allies on the day of the meeting, but it was too late for further fighting. Tsar Alexander agreed to the terms that Francis had approved, which required the Russian army to return home. This they happily did, leaving the Austrians alone to negotiate for their occupied country as best they could.

The meeting between Napoleon and Francis at Spálény mill on 4 December. Accompanied by Prince Liechtenstein, Francis concluded an armistice with Napoleon that brought a final end to the fighting.

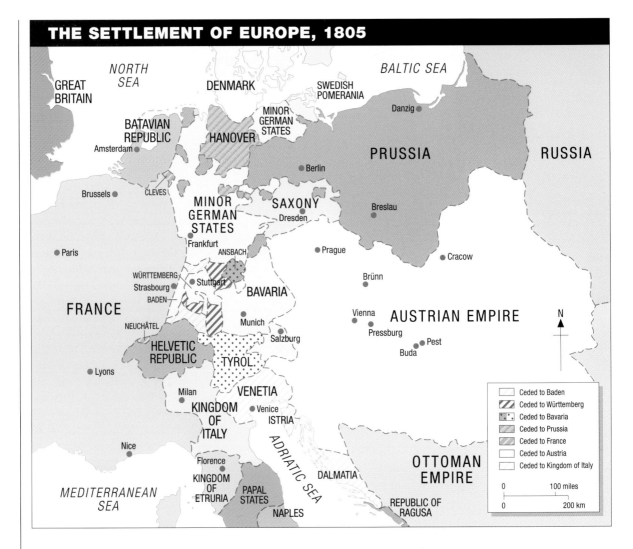

THE SETTLEMENT OF EUROPE, 1805

NORTH SEA

GREAT BRITAIN

DENMARK

BALTIC SEA

SWEDISH POMERANIA

Danzig

BATAVIAN REPUBLIC

Amsterdam

HANOVER

MINOR GERMAN STATES

PRUSSIA

RUSSIA

Berlin

Brussels

CLEVES

MINOR GERMAN STATES

SAXONY

Dresden

Breslau

Frankfurt

ANSBACH

Prague

Cracow

Paris

WÜRTTEMBERG

Strasbourg

BADEN

Stuttgart

BAVARIA

Brünn

FRANCE

NEUCHÂTEL

Munich

Vienna

Pressburg

AUSTRIAN EMPIRE

N

Salzburg

Pest

Buda

HELVETIC REPUBLIC

TYROL

Lyons

Milan

VENETIA

KINGDOM OF ITALY

Venice

ISTRIA

ADRIATIC SEA

DALMATIA

OTTOMAN EMPIRE

Nice

Florence

KINGDOM OF ETRURIA

PAPAL STATES

MEDITERRANEAN SEA

NAPLES

REPUBLIC OF RAGUSA

	Ceded to Baden
	Ceded to Württemberg
	Ceded to Bavaria
	Ceded to Prussia
	Ceded to France
	Ceded to Austria
	Ceded to Kingdom of Italy

0 — 100 miles
0 — 200 km

The talks that followed saw Austria suffer greatly for her part in the war. The Treaty of Pressburg, signed on 27 December 1805, decreed that Austria would lose her provinces of Dalmatia, Istria and Venice to Napoleon's new Kingdom of Italy, and Bavaria would gain the Tyrol and Vorarlberg in reward for its support. Baden and Württemberg gained territory too, while Austria suffered the further humiliation of a 40 million Franc indemnity. With this further weakening of Austria's influence in the German territories, the sickly Holy Roman Empire was finally dissolved the following year, paving the way for the creation of the Confederation of the Rhine. Prussia had been close to intervention in the war when the Battle of Austerlitz changed everything. Napoleon extracted certain guarantees from Prussia allowing him free rein in southern Germany and Italy while forcing them to cede Ansbach to Bavaria and two other small principalities to France. However, he sweetened the pill for Prussia by handing over the long-coveted territory of Hanover.

While the Austrians and Russians had been marching to defeat at Austerlitz the supporting attacks that made up the Allies' grand strategy had also come to nothing. The landing in southern Italy was greatly

A French dragoon escorts a wounded Austrian prisoner into captivity. Allied losses were massive; in the region of 29,000 men. The Russians lost about 16,000 killed or wounded, the Austrians some 600 killed and 1,200 wounded. Prisoners taken amounted to about 9,500 Russians and 1,670 Austrians. Total French losses are put at 8,800, with about 1,290 reported killed, 6,990 wounded and 570 captured, although this may be an underestimate. (Girbal – Sammlung Alfred und Roland Umhey)

delayed. By the time it took place Austerlitz had been fought and lost, forcing the British and Russians to abandon their mission. Similarly, delays negated other efforts by British, Swedish and Russian forces. Austerlitz left the Third Coalition in tatters and it ceased to exist. Austria was left with a festering bitterness as a result of the indignities Napoleon imposed on her and would take the field against the French emperor again in 1809. Prussia fought a campaign against Napoleon in 1806, suffering a crushing defeat at the twin battles of Jena and Auerstadt in October. Russia suffered a similar fate at Friedland in June 1807.

Austerlitz had been a stunning victory for Napoleon. His army, honed to perfection at the camps on the Channel coast, had outmanoeuvred the clumsy, unco-ordinated efforts of the Allies. The control of the Allied army became compromised by the presence of Tsar Alexander, who, assuming supreme command, then allowed the overconfidence of his inexperienced advisors to seduce him. As a result, Napoleon was able to draw the Allied army into battle on ground he had chosen in advance. The complicated Allied plan required a close co-ordination that was beyond the capabilities of the joint armies and left it exposed to the counterstroke Napoleon had already planned for the centre. It is testimony to the skilled and tireless manoeuvring of the French army, in particular St. Hilaire and Vandamme's divisions of Soult's IV Corps, that after the battle Alexander believed the Allies were beaten because the French had formed superior numbers at all the crucial points on the battlefield. Yet it was these two divisions that had between them stormed the Pratzen plateau, defeated IV Column, faced an attack by the Russian Imperial Guard, attacked the retreating Russians at Augezd and marched on the rear of II and III Columns at Sokolnitz.

It is fascinating to consider that there probably would not have been a Battle of Austerlitz had the Tsar not been present. Kutuzov made it clear he was in favour of retiring further, playing for time, but was overruled. Reinforced by Archduke Charles's army from Italy and with the imminent promised intervention of Prussia, he could have returned

A French cartoon of the death of William Pitt. The devil is carrying Pitt down to hell, snapping the reins on George III, who is falling towards the chasm over a sack marked 'Depot of crimes of the English Government'. Some said the news of Austerlitz had killed Pitt.

to the offensive against a French army exposed at the end of a long supply line in country cleared of food and forage by the Allies. The outcome may have been very different from that at Austerlitz.

For the local population the battlefield was an indescribable horror: On 4 December they began to return to their shattered homes. Inside they found, 'stiff corpses and dying emaciated people, some of whom were trying to push their wounded insides back into their broken torsos'. Two days later they were ordered to drag all the dead horses from the Satschan pond and recovered somewhere between 130 and 150; of human bodies they only found two or three more to add to the 200 or so that had been dragged out on the day of battle. Napoleon's statement in his famous 30th Bulletin that 20,000 Russians had drowned in the ponds was pure propaganda. In addition, probably around 30 artillery pieces were recovered after the pond was drained. On 8 December, six days after the battle, the villagers from Satschan ventured on to the battlefield. One man, shocked by what he saw, wrote there were 'thousands of corpses' amongst which there was 'a hand lying here, a leg lying there, a decapitated body, a torso. There was a horribly disfigured man who raised his bloody hand toward us, crying for help. There was another one who was digging deep into his own infected wounds, frozen up to his hips in mud, pleading with us, in his despair, to kill him.'

News of Napoleon's great victory did not reach London until the last days of the year. When he first heard the news William Pitt, the British Prime Minister, architect of the Third Coalition and 'saviour of Europe', was devastated. Turning to a map of Europe hung on the wall he prophetically announced, 'Roll up that map; it will not be wanted these ten years'. Never a well man, Pitt took to his bed and on 16 January 1806 he died. Many said he too was a victim of the Battle of Austerlitz.

THE BATTLEFIELD TODAY

Although almost 200 years have passed since the Eagles of France, Russia and Austria clashed on the cold and frosty fields of Moravia, large parts of the battlefield are unchanged by time. In 1992 the Czech government declared the battlefield a national historic site, which hopefully will guarantee it remains this way for future generations.

The battlefield can be explored in a day and a reasonable overview gained, but if you wish to visit the museums and Slavkov castle too, then a little more time may be required. It is important to note that the traditionally familiar names of the villages have changed. The former German names are now represented in their Czech form. The following list may prove useful.

Original rendition	Current rendition
Austerlitz	Slavkov u Brna
Augezd	Újezd u Brna
Blasowitz	Blazovice
Bosenitz	Tvarozná
Brünn	Brno
Holubitz	Holubice
Jirzikowitz	Jirikovice
Kobelnitz	Kobylnice
Krug	Kruh
Krzenowitz	Krenovice
Olmütz	Olomouc
Puntowitz	Ponetovice
Pratze	Prace
Satschan	Zatcany
Slapanitz	Slapanice
Sokolnitz	Sokolnice
Telnitz	Telnice

The nearest large town to use as a base is Brno although it is only a two-hour drive from the Austrian capital of Vienna. From Brno there is now a major highway that cuts across the northern flank of the battlefield, running parallel with the old Brünn–Olmütz road. When approaching the battlefield white roadsigns bearing silhouettes of three soldiers and the names Santon, Zuran or Mohyla Miru (Peace Monument) indicate where to turn off on to the old road (the 430). The route you follow around the battlefield is obviously one of personal choice, but as a starting point you may wish to follow the path I took.

From the junction with the main highway, follow the sign to the Zuran, the hill where Napoleon had his headquarters for the first part of the battle. There is a distinctive tree marking the site, a small parking area and a relief map of the battlefield. From here the visitor can appreciate the vast size of the battlefield for the first time. By retracing your route back to the highway, and crossing it, you will come to the Santon, the hill on which Napoleon anchored the left of his position.

Leaving your car in Tvarozna (Bosenitz) follow one of the stepped footpaths to the top of the Santon from where there are excellent views across the northern end of the battlefield. Over this wide expanse of farmland spread out before you, Lannes led his two divisions towards Bagration's Russian forces. In Tvarozna, within the building which houses the post office and local government offices, there is a diorama of the battle. Driving back to the 430, turn left and follow the road to the Stará Posta (old post office). This recently restored building played a prominent role in the battle. On the morning of 2 December it served as Bagration's headquarters, but that evening Napoleon slept there after his meeting with Johann Liechtenstein. The buildings now hosts a restaurant, wine cellar and small museum.

Retrace your route back along the 430 and take the left turn towards Blazovice. The gently undulating ground either side of the road is where the French and Russian cavalry fought out their desperate battles. From Blazovice follow the road southwards, cross the railway and wind gently up to the highpoint of Staré Vinohrady (old vineyard) to where IR23 fought Vandamme's men, passing the site of the battle of the Russian Imperial Guard on the way. Return to Blazovice, head towards Jirikovice, and ponder the attack of Soult's corps on the Pratzen plateau. If you stop between Blazovice and Jirikovice and look to the left of the road you will observe the country traversed by Vandamme and St. Hilaire. Once at Jirikovice turn towards Ponetovice and following the road you will be in the area where these two divisions deployed in low ground prior to their attack. From here the value of this ground is clear, as it is well hidden from any prying eyes on the Pratzen. A road leading from Ponetovice to Prace follows the line taken by St. Hilaire's men when they attacked the village. At Prace follow the signs to the Mohyla Miru (Peace

A photograph taken from the Santon hill looking towards the village of Bosenitz (now Tvarozná). A reproduction French 8-pdr gun stands on the summit of the Santon close to a chapel, built in 1832, to replace the one destroyed in 1805

Monument). Completed in 1912, this dramatic monument houses a chapel, beneath which is an ossuary containing bones of some of those killed in battle. There is also a museum behind the monument. The monument, built on the Pratzeberg, marks the site of the vicious fighting between St. Hilaire, Kamensky and Kolowrat. Unfortunately the degree to which this part of the battlefield can be explored is limited by the fenced-off area around a radar/transmitting station built on the site.

From the monument, turn left out of the car park and follow the road to the southern end of the plateau, from where you can look down across the vineyards to the villages of Ujezd, Zatcany, Telnice and Sokolnice. Of the ponds that were so significant in the later stages of the battle there is no longer any trace. You can either continue on the road down towards Telnice or return towards Mohyla Miru and take a left turn, which leads directly down to the wall of the pheasantry at Sokolnice. Along the wall of the pheasantry are marks traditionally claiming to show the positions of a French artillery battery, however, I have found no evidence that suggests the French held this eastern side of the pheasantry at any time in the battle. Continuing southwards, the village of Sokolnice contains the heavily restored castle that saw so much fighting, a vast granary barn and a number of other period buildings. Beyond Sokolnice lay the villages of Telnice, which saw heavy fighting, Zatcany, marking the southern side of the great pond, now replaced by open farmland, and finally Ujezd, from where the first advance to battle took place. Above this village, hidden amongst the private gardens and allotments of the villagers, is the Chapel of St. Antonin. Built in 1863 this chapel replaced the original one, destroyed in 1814. It was from this spot that Napoleon watched as the Russians attempted to escape across the frozen ice at the end of the battle.

No tour would be complete without a visit to Slavkov (Austerlitz). Slavkov castle and its beautiful grounds belonged to the Kaunitz family. Within the space of a few days either side of the battle, the castle was home to three Emperors, Alexander, Francis and Napoleon.

For anyone planning a visit to Austerlitz there is an excellent internet site at www.austerlitz-region.cz which provides much useful information in English, French and Czech.

FURTHER READING

For a battle as significant as Austerlitz there have been relatively few books written in English specifically analysing the campaign and the final action on 2 December 1805. Most writers until recently relied very heavily on French accounts, often ignoring Austrian and Russian sources entirely. This has inevitably given an unbalanced view on the history of this campaign. Probably the most well known and readily available book on the subject is Christopher Duffy's *Austerlitz 1805* (London, 1977 and recently republished in paperback). Duffy was the first to attempt to redress this imbalance. Colonel F.N. Maude's *The Ulm Campaign 1805* (London, 1912) has, I believe, never been reprinted, which is a great pity as this is a fascinating detailed examination of the early part of the 1805 campaign. Maude has interesting comments to make on the geography of the area, which adversely affected the movements of the Austrian army, and offers an insight into Mack's thinking. The reprinting of Major-General Stutterheim's *A Detailed Account of the Battle of Austerlitz* (London 1807; reprinted Cambridge, 1985) has made readily available much useful information on the Allied version of events.

Colonel G.A. Furse's *The Campaigns of 1805: Ulm, Trafalgar, Austerlitz* (1905; reprinted Tyne & Wear 1995) was one of the first English accounts of the campaign and contains much useful information although it should not be read in isolation. Furse included a detailed appendix pulling together all the research disproving Napoleon's claim of vast Allied casualties in the frozen ponds. Claude Manceron's *Austerlitz* (Paris, 1963, reprinted London, 1966) is an interesting read but in reality is a fictionalised account of the battle, very much from a French viewpoint. Captain F.W.O. Maycock's *The Napoleonic Campaign of 1805* (Aldershot, 1912) was initially written for army officers and is a general overview of the campaign. The most recent work to cover the subject is Scott Bowden's *Napoleon and Austerlitz – 'The Glory Years' of 1805–1807* (Chicago, 1997). Bowden has continued the trend set by Duffy by attempting to bring the Allied viewpoint more to the fore, although I understand some questions have been raised as to whether all the Russian and Austrian sources quoted have actually been consulted.

INDEX